STEPHEN BIESTY'S
INCREDIBLE
CROSS-SECTIONS

ILLUSTRATED BY
STEPHEN BIESTY

WRITTEN BY
RICHARD PLATT

DORLING KINDERSLEY
LONDON • NEW YORK • STUTTGART

DK

A DORLING KINDERSLEY BOOK

Project Editor John C. Miles
Art Editor Richard Czapnik
Production Marguerite Fenn
Managing Editor Ann Kramer
Art Director Roger Priddy

First published in 1992 by Dorling Kindersley Limited,
9 Henrietta Street, London WC2E 8PS

Reprinted 1992, 1993

A CIP catalogue record for this book is available
from the British Library.

ISBN 0-86318-807-9

Reproduced by Dot Gradations, Essex
Printed and bound in Italy by A. Mondadori Editore, Verona

CONTENTS

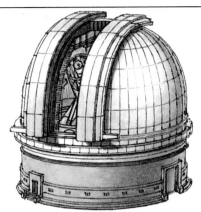

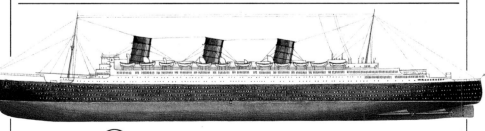

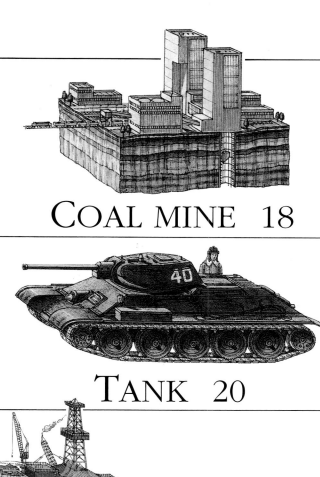

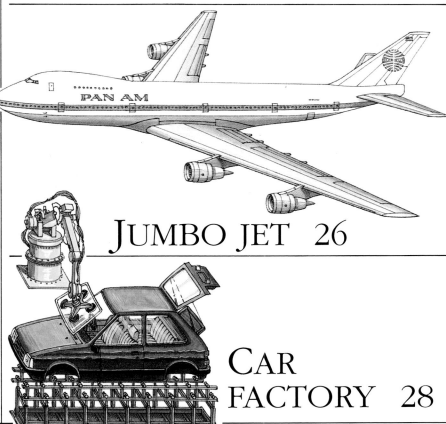

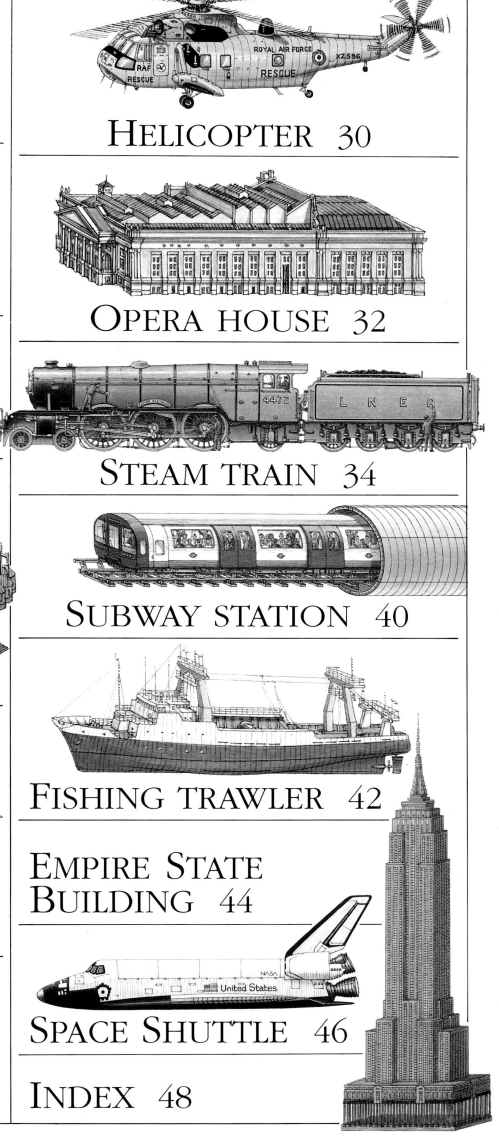

CASTLE

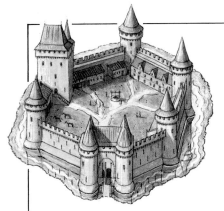

Many 14th-century castles had thick outer walls, which enclosed a central open area.

Hundreds of years ago, life in Europe was dangerous, and wars were common. So powerful people built castles — strong homes where they could shelter from their enemies, or launch attacks against them. Usually a nobleman, or lord, owned the castle. The king gave the lord land in return for soldiers to help fight wars. Tenants farmed the lord's land. In return for their labour, they earned enough to live on and were protected in wartime by the lord and his soldiers. Society inside the castle walls mirrored the world outside. The lord and his officials managed the castle and the lands around it. Below the officials there were priests, important servants, and soldiers. At the bottom of castle society were the most humble workers, such as labourers and the cesspit cleaner shown below.

Deadly fire
Narrow slits in the castle walls allowed archers to fire freely, while protecting them from incoming arrows. The overhang at the top of the walls meant that the castle defenders could drop stones on attackers' heads to stop them climbing the walls.

Gatehouse
The only way into the castle was through the gatehouse. This was the weakest point in the castle wall. Defenders on the top of the wall fired arrows at attackers who got too close, or threw boiling water down on them. The defenders could also lower a huge gate, called a portcullis, which trapped the attackers.

Getting inside
Capturing a castle was difficult. Attackers had to try to tunnel under the walls, trick the people inside, or lay siege and starve them out to gain access. Castles were an effective defence until about 350 years ago, when gunpowder came into wide use and attacking armies could easily blow holes in the strongest castle wall.

A moat point
Another defence was a water-filled trench called a moat, which surrounded the castle. The moat was a difficult hurdle for attackers, and also stopped them digging a tunnel under the walls. The road to the gatehouse crossed the moat by a hinged drawbridge which could be raised in seconds.

Doing time
Prisoners were locked up in an underground cell, called a dungeon. Oubliettes, or secret dungeons, got their name from the French word, *oublier*, to forget. Oubliettes were reserved for the most hated prisoners. Their captors locked them in the oubliette — and forgot about them!

Commander's quarters

Tiled roof

Castle guards

Food store

Portcullis

Drawbridge

CASTLE PERSONALITIES

Cesspit cleaner

Priest

Noble family

Jester

Knight

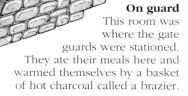

On guard
This room was where the gate guards were stationed. They ate their meals here and warmed themselves by a basket of hot charcoal called a brazier.

The keep
The keep was the strongest and largest tower in the castle. It contained the private rooms of the noble family as well as the Great Hall. The centre of castle society was the Great Hall. This was where everyone gathered to eat and to watch entertainers such as musicians or jugglers.

Rub-a-dub-dub
During a siege, water was precious. Only the noble family bathed often.

Bailiff's room
In this room an official called the bailiff ran the lord's estates and counted and stored his treasure.

Solar comfort
A castle was a home as well as a fortress, so there were private rooms for the noble family. The solar was a private drawing room which may also have been used as a bedroom. It was usually the best room in the castle, with comfortable furnishings and a large window.

Private worship
The noble family had a chapel where they worshipped.

Chapel altar

Great Hall

Chimneys
The oldest castles were very smokey places, as smoke from fires only escaped through a hole in the roof. Chimneys, which worked better, were introduced in the 14th century.

Battlements

A walk on the wall
Along the top of the castle wall was a path called a wall-walk. It enabled defending soldiers to move quickly around the castle to the point of attack. Stone pillars, or battlements, protected soldiers on the wall-walk from enemy arrows.

Cistern
Rainwater from the roofs drained into huge stone tanks called cisterns. Lead pipes took the water to the kitchen.

Wooden shutter
Window glass was not widely used until the 15th century, making castles very cold places.

Deadly tubes
Soldiers used artillery (heavy guns) from the middle of the 14th century. The first cannons were just tubes of metal fixed to stout wooden frames.

Cheers!
Everyone drank strong beer with meals — even the "small beer" that children drank was more alcoholic than beer is today. Beer was brewed often, because until hops were used in brewing in the 15th century, beer did not keep well.

Fermenting beer

Splash!
The toilets in castles were called garderobes. They were very primitive. Usually there was just a hole that led to the outside wall. Sewage from some of the garderobes went straight into the moat.

Exit from garderobe

Forging links
At the forge the armourer manufactured and repaired weapons and armour, and the farrier (blacksmith) made and fitted horseshoes.

Clever defence
Steps of the staircase always rose clockwise. This gave a defending soldier an advantage as he retreated up the stairs: holding his sword in his right hand, he could swing it freely. But the centre-post blocked the attacker's sword hand.

Well, well...
Castles needed lots of fresh water, so there was a deep well to supply the inhabitants.

Stables

Centre-post

Open hearth
There was no cooker in the kitchen. The cooks roasted meat in front of an open fire, and boiled food in huge pots.

Salt meat
Meat was salted to preserve it.

Food storage
To survive a siege, the castle inhabitants needed lots of food. Stores included hundreds of sacks of grain, which was made into flour for bread. The coolest part of the castle was the cellar, so perishable food was stored there.

Solid foundations
The castle walls were thickest at the bottom, where they were most at risk from tunnelling by enemy miners. Only the shell of the castle wall was made from trimmed stones. Rubble filled the core of the castle wall.

This job's the pits...
Other garderobes in many parts of the castle emptied into cesspits. Cleaning them out was a very smelly job!

OBSERVATORY

How far can you see? Pick up a telescope, and you can see mountains on the Moon, nearly 400,000 kilometres away. The Hale telescope at Mount Palomar, in the United States, is so powerful that it is never pointed at anything as close as the Moon. Instead, astronomers (people who study the stars) use it to look at far more distant objects in the night sky. The telescope's 5-metre wide mirror can detect stars too distant for our eyes to see. Some of these stars are so far away that their light takes millions of years to reach the Earth. Looking at these stars is like looking into the past, for you are seeing them as they were millions of years ago.

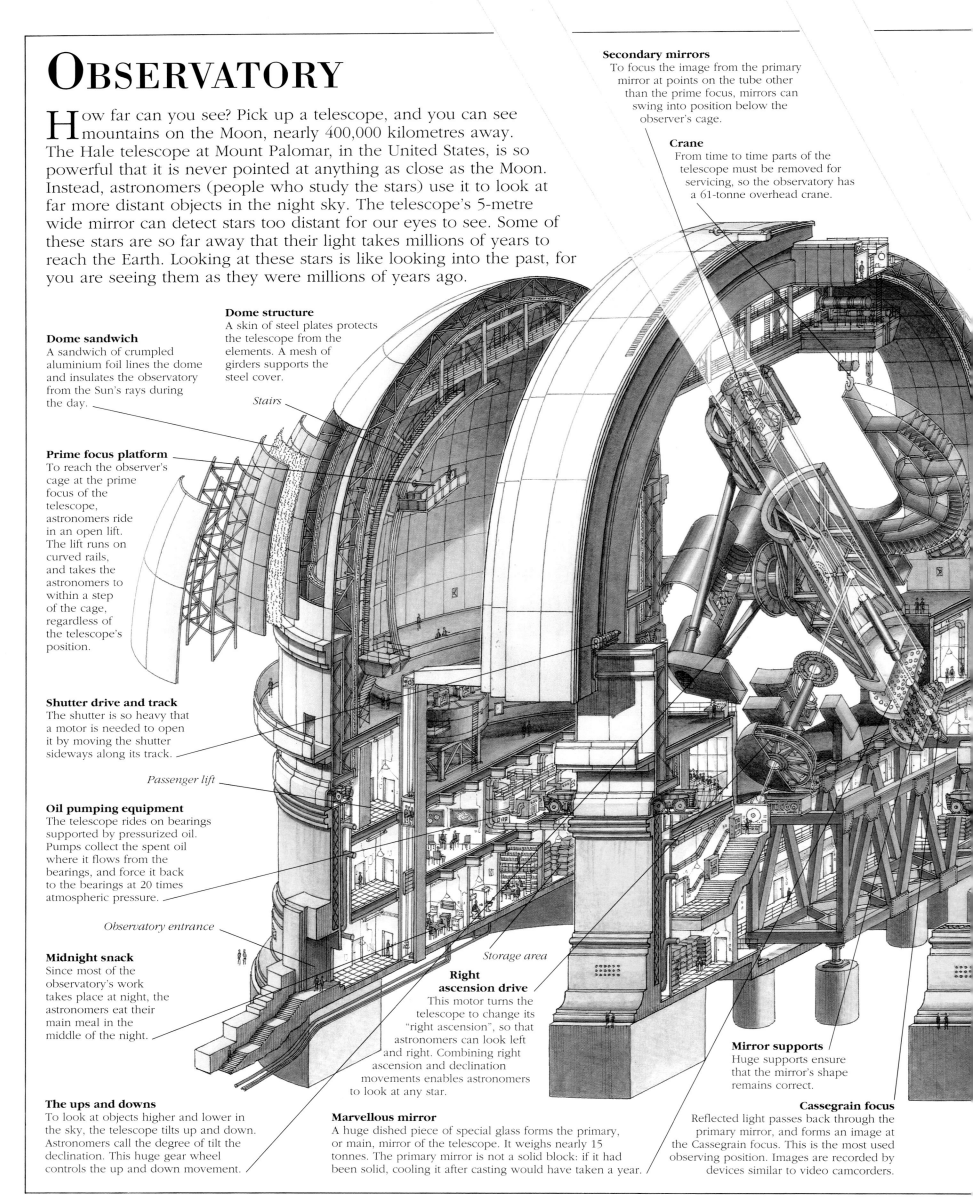

Dome sandwich
A sandwich of crumpled aluminium foil lines the dome and insulates the observatory from the Sun's rays during the day.

Dome structure
A skin of steel plates protects the telescope from the elements. A mesh of girders supports the steel cover.

Stairs

Prime focus platform
To reach the observer's cage at the prime focus of the telescope, astronomers ride in an open lift. The lift runs on curved rails, and takes the astronomers to within a step of the cage, regardless of the telescope's position.

Shutter drive and track
The shutter is so heavy that a motor is needed to open it by moving the shutter sideways along its track.

Passenger lift

Oil pumping equipment
The telescope rides on bearings supported by pressurized oil. Pumps collect the spent oil where it flows from the bearings, and force it back to the bearings at 20 times atmospheric pressure.

Observatory entrance

Midnight snack
Since most of the observatory's work takes place at night, the astronomers eat their main meal in the middle of the night.

The ups and downs
To look at objects higher and lower in the sky, the telescope tilts up and down. Astronomers call the degree of tilt the declination. This huge gear wheel controls the up and down movement.

Secondary mirrors
To focus the image from the primary mirror at points on the tube other than the prime focus, mirrors can swing into position below the observer's cage.

Crane
From time to time parts of the telescope must be removed for servicing, so the observatory has a 61-tonne overhead crane.

Storage area

Right ascension drive
This motor turns the telescope to change its "right ascension", so that astronomers can look left and right. Combining right ascension and declination movements enables astronomers to look at any star.

Marvellous mirror
A huge dished piece of special glass forms the primary, or main, mirror of the telescope. It weighs nearly 15 tonnes. The primary mirror is not a solid block: if it had been solid, cooling it after casting would have taken a year.

Mirror supports
Huge supports ensure that the mirror's shape remains correct.

Cassegrain focus
Reflected light passes back through the primary mirror, and forms an image at the Cassegrain focus. This is the most used observing position. Images are recorded by devices similar to video camcorders.

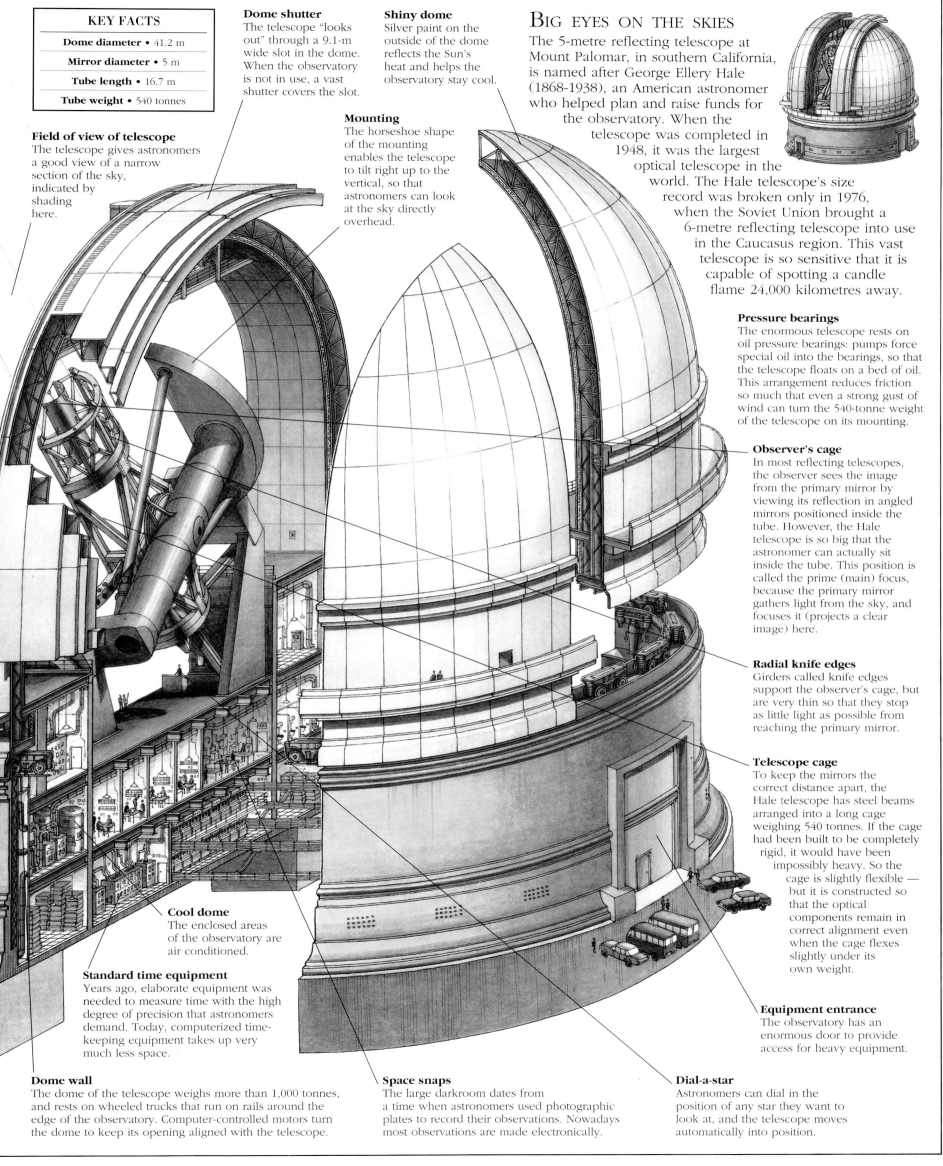

KEY FACTS

Dome diameter • 41.2 m	
Mirror diameter • 5 m	
Tube length • 16.7 m	
Tube weight • 540 tonnes	

Dome shutter
The telescope "looks out" through a 9.1-m wide slot in the dome. When the observatory is not in use, a vast shutter covers the slot.

Shiny dome
Silver paint on the outside of the dome reflects the Sun's heat and helps the observatory stay cool.

Field of view of telescope
The telescope gives astronomers a good view of a narrow section of the sky, indicated by shading here.

Mounting
The horseshoe shape of the mounting enables the telescope to tilt right up to the vertical, so that astronomers can look at the sky directly overhead.

BIG EYES ON THE SKIES

The 5-metre reflecting telescope at Mount Palomar, in southern California, is named after George Ellery Hale (1868-1938), an American astronomer who helped plan and raise funds for the observatory. When the telescope was completed in 1948, it was the largest optical telescope in the world. The Hale telescope's size record was broken only in 1976, when the Soviet Union brought a 6-metre reflecting telescope into use in the Caucasus region. This vast telescope is so sensitive that it is capable of spotting a candle flame 24,000 kilometres away.

Pressure bearings
The enormous telescope rests on oil pressure bearings: pumps force special oil into the bearings, so that the telescope floats on a bed of oil. This arrangement reduces friction so much that even a strong gust of wind can turn the 540-tonne weight of the telescope on its mounting.

Observer's cage
In most reflecting telescopes, the observer sees the image from the primary mirror by viewing its reflection in angled mirrors positioned inside the tube. However, the Hale telescope is so big that the astronomer can actually sit inside the tube. This position is called the prime (main) focus, because the primary mirror gathers light from the sky, and focuses it (projects a clear image) here.

Radial knife edges
Girders called knife edges support the observer's cage, but are very thin so that they stop as little light as possible from reaching the primary mirror.

Telescope cage
To keep the mirrors the correct distance apart, the Hale telescope has steel beams arranged into a long cage weighing 540 tonnes. If the cage had been built to be completely rigid, it would have been impossibly heavy. So the cage is slightly flexible — but it is constructed so that the optical components remain in correct alignment even when the cage flexes slightly under its own weight.

Equipment entrance
The observatory has an enormous door to provide access for heavy equipment.

Cool dome
The enclosed areas of the observatory are air conditioned.

Standard time equipment
Years ago, elaborate equipment was needed to measure time with the high degree of precision that astronomers demand. Today, computerized time-keeping equipment takes up very much less space.

Dome wall
The dome of the telescope weighs more than 1,000 tonnes, and rests on wheeled trucks that run on rails around the edge of the observatory. Computer-controlled motors turn the dome to keep its opening aligned with the telescope.

Space snaps
The large darkroom dates from a time when astronomers used photographic plates to record their observations. Nowadays most observations are made electronically.

Dial-a-star
Astronomers can dial in the position of any star they want to look at, and the telescope moves automatically into position.

GALLEON

In the 16th century, large ships regularly set off across the blue Caribbean, carrying the plundered riches of the Americas back to Spain. With their billowing sails and creaking timbers, these galleons looked and sounded beautiful. But what would it have been like for the sailors? The first thing they would have noticed when they went on board was the smell — a mixture of tar, bad drains, and sweat. With a daily water ration of little more than one litre, there was not much left for washing. The ship was very crowded; there was no privacy, because every bit of space was needed for stores and equipment. Huge rats scuttled in the shadows, and the ship was infested with fleas. The food tasted disgusting, and most of the crew were constantly seasick. With a good wind, the journey from the Americas to Spain took more than two months. If the ship was becalmed (reached a patch of sea with no wind) or ran into rough weather, the journey could take even longer.

Jardines
For lavatories, the crew used seats overhanging the deck rail. As a joke they called them jardines — a French word meaning gardens.

Place your bets
Many sailors gambled, betting on cards, dice, or almost anything that involved chance. Life on board ship for months at a time was very dull, and the ship's crew welcomed any activity which filled the long hours off-duty.

Swivel guns
These small guns were nicknamed "murderers". They were used against enemy sailors.

Tunes
Singing special songs called shanties helped the sailors work. The songs had a strong rhythm which helped the sailors to all heave at the same time.

It's about time
Everyone in the crew took turns at the watch (keeping look-out). Watches lasted eight hours, and were timed with an hour glass. Sand took half an hour to run through the narrow waist of this glass bottle.

Gratings
Structures called gratings let in light and air to the lower decks. They also let in lots of water.

Deck rail

Anchors aweigh!
The anchor cable ran around a huge drum called a capstan. The sailors turned the drum to raise the anchor.

Ram
The carved figure on the bow (front) of the ship could be used to ram enemy ships.

Soldiers
On Spanish fighting ships, the crew simply sailed the vessel, and did not fight. Infantry (soldiers) operated the guns and attacked the enemy.

Stowaways
Thousands of rats lived on board ship. In 1622, the sailors on one ship killed 4,000 rats during the voyage from the Caribbean to Europe. The rats that survived ate most of the ship's food.

Sacks of food

Food storage
Ships carried olive oil for cooking in huge jars. Normally meat was pickled in salt water but it was also preserved by hanging it from the deck rail in the salt spray. On one 17th century voyage sharks snapped at the meat dangling above the water!

Hull
The hull, or main body of the ship, was made entirely out of wood. It took hundreds of trees to build a really big wooden ship.

KEY FACTS
Length • 43 m
Keel length • 30 m
Beam (width) • 11 m
Weight • 500 tonnes
Armament • 24 cannon firing 14 kg balls, 30 cannon firing 8 kg balls, 2 swivel guns

An even keel
The keel was the backbone of the ship, and helped it sail in a straight line. To stay upright, the ship carried ballast in the hold (storage area). Rocks and cannon balls made good ballast.

Water, water everywhere...
Everyone on board was allowed only 1.1 litres of water every day, or twice this amount of beer or cider. Every ship had to carry enough fresh water for the whole voyage, because sea water contains too much salt to drink.

Food and cooking
Each day every member of the crew ate only 700 g of biscuits and 250 g of dried meat or fish. Some days they ate a dish of beans or peas as well. By the end of a long voyage much of the food had gone bad, and the biscuits were filled with insects. When the sea was too rough, cooking was impossible, so the crew ate cheese instead of meat or fish.

Heave ho!
Everyone suffered from seasickness, even old sailors. Lemons were thought to be a cure, but were probably useless.

Please, God...
Spanish seamen say "He who goes to sea learns how to pray". A sea voyage could be terrifying, and people prayed that they would arrive safely.

Mainmast

Sew what
When sails became torn the crew had to repair them by hand. Sails that were badly damaged were sometimes used for shrouds to wrap the bodies of sailors who died. Weighted with rocks, the body sank.

Livestock
Many ships carried pigs, sheep, and chickens. Fresh eggs and meat were reserved for the sick and the ship's most senior officers.

Sleeping
Sailors on the ship did not have cabins. They just slept wherever there was space.

What's that?
The crew looked at distant objects with a telescope, which made the objects appear bigger.

Large lantern

Decoration
The sterns (rear ends) of 17th-century sailing ships were painted in bright colours and had carved decoration. There were also big lanterns so other ships could see them at night.

Captain's cabin
The captain's cabin was the largest and most comfortable on the ship.

Treasure chests
Spanish ships returning from South America and the Caribbean often carried precious cargoes of gold. A strong chest kept the treasure safe during the voyage.

Lanterns
Strict regulations controlled the use of candles, because of the risk of fire.

Hinged gunport

At the helm
The helmsman steered the ship using a whipstaff — a long pole attached to the tiller. The tiller itself turned the rudder.

Big shots
Heavy carriage guns fired cannon balls (made of metal or stone), grape shot (lumps of lead the size of grapes) or pieces of metal which destroyed the rigging of enemy ships.

Whipstaff

Tiller

Barrels of gunpowder

Rudder

Mind the gap
Ropes soaked in tar were used to seal the gaps between planks.

The galley
Cooking facilities were different on every ship. Often there was no chimney, so the kitchen (called a galley at sea) got very smokey.

Ballast

A sting in the bale
Poisonous scorpions often lurked in the cargoes of wood that were carried in the hold.

A real pong
Seawater that seeped into the ship collected in the bilge — the space between the hold and the keel — and turned into a foul brew. This pump cleared the bilges, but the smell of the water was disgusting.

Spares
Damage to the rigging (the sails and ropes) was common, so every ship carried spares. Rats ate even the sails if they could, so spare sails were often stored in empty barrels.

NEW HORIZONS
In the 16th century, Spanish shipyards began to build a new kind of warship called a galleon. It was based on an earlier design called a carrack, but was narrower and more manoeuvrable. Naval guns had become powerful and accurate, and galleons were designed to use them effectively.

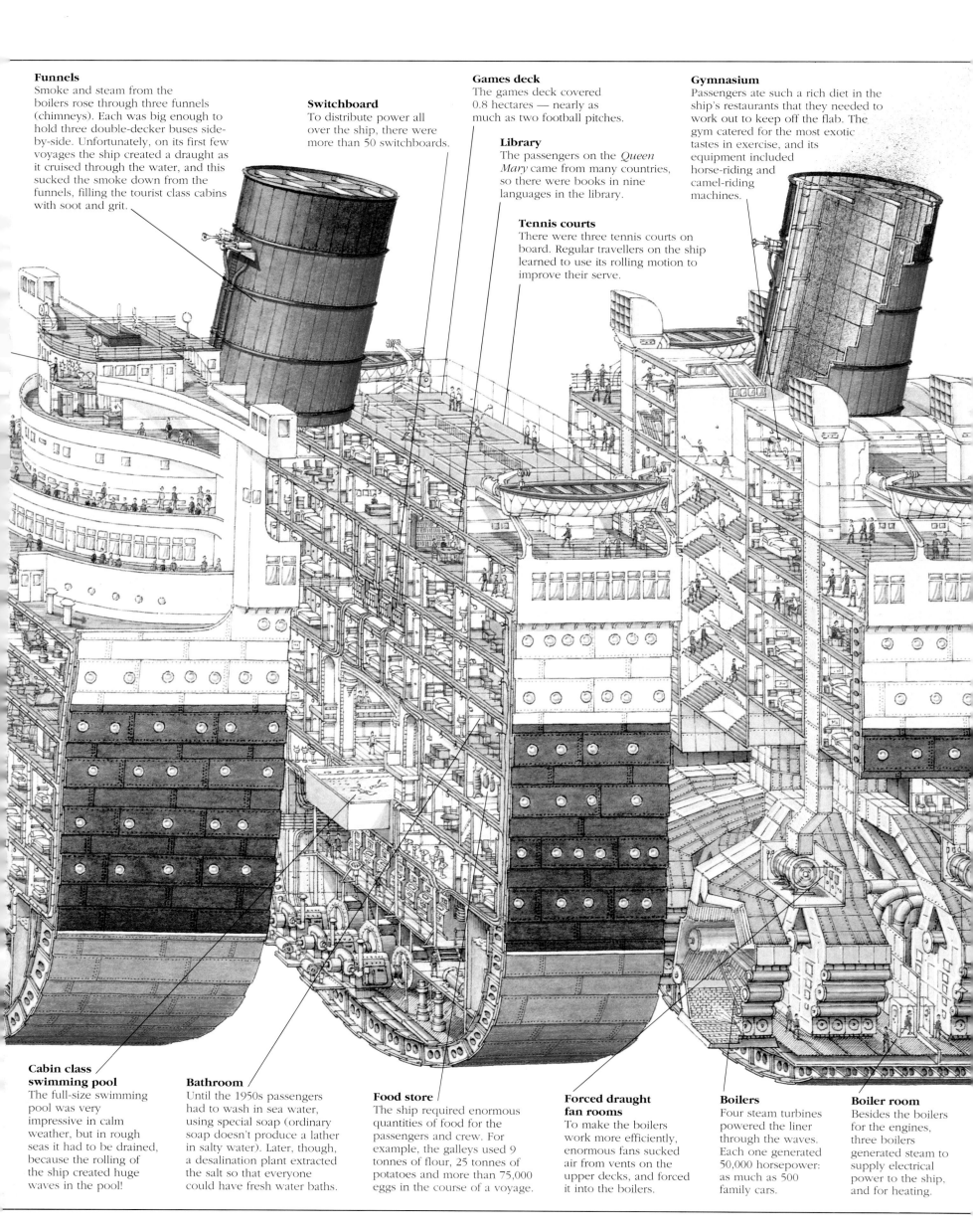

Funnels
Smoke and steam from the boilers rose through three funnels (chimneys). Each was big enough to hold three double-decker buses side-by-side. Unfortunately, on its first few voyages the ship created a draught as it cruised through the water, and this sucked the smoke down from the funnels, filling the tourist class cabins with soot and grit.

Switchboard
To distribute power all over the ship, there were more than 50 switchboards.

Games deck
The games deck covered 0.8 hectares — nearly as much as two football pitches.

Library
The passengers on the *Queen Mary* came from many countries, so there were books in nine languages in the library.

Tennis courts
There were three tennis courts on board. Regular travellers on the ship learned to use its rolling motion to improve their serve.

Gymnasium
Passengers ate such a rich diet in the ship's restaurants that they needed to work out to keep off the flab. The gym catered for the most exotic tastes in exercise, and its equipment included horse-riding and camel-riding machines.

Cabin class swimming pool
The full-size swimming pool was very impressive in calm weather, but in rough seas it had to be drained, because the rolling of the ship created huge waves in the pool!

Bathroom
Until the 1950s passengers had to wash in sea water, using special soap (ordinary soap doesn't produce a lather in salty water). Later, though, a desalination plant extracted the salt so that everyone could have fresh water baths.

Food store
The ship required enormous quantities of food for the passengers and crew. For example, the galleys used 9 tonnes of flour, 25 tonnes of potatoes and more than 75,000 eggs in the course of a voyage.

Forced draught fan rooms
To make the boilers work more efficiently, enormous fans sucked air from vents on the upper decks, and forced it into the boilers.

Boilers
Four steam turbines powered the liner through the waves. Each one generated 50,000 horsepower: as much as 500 family cars.

Boiler room
Besides the boilers for the engines, three boilers generated steam to supply electrical power to the ship, and for heating.

OCEAN LINER

Crossing the Atlantic Ocean today in a supersonic airliner requires just a few hours of considerable discomfort, but in 1936 things were different. Travelling between Britain and New York meant a sea voyage lasting at least four days — only the most daring flew.

Shipping companies of the time competed to provide their passengers with the fastest, most luxurious crossing. It was this competition that led to the construction of the *Queen Mary*. When this enormous ship was built, she was the fastest passenger liner in the world, and probably the most luxurious. The ship's owners, the Cunard Line, spent millions to create a vast floating hotel as good as any found on land.

The *Queen Mary* had three classes of passengers, just like the First, Club, and Tourist classes on an airliner. Cabin class passengers had suites of rooms with fresh flowers, and adjoining cabins for their servants. Tourist class passengers had less fancy rooms, but they still travelled in some style. Third class passengers paid the least for their tickets, and they got plain cabins in the noisiest, smokiest part of the ship.

However, the Atlantic wind and waves did not know or care how much each passenger had paid for a ticket. Those in Cabin and Third class suffered equally from seasickness. And how they suffered! Nobody had built a ship as big as the *Queen Mary* before, and her designers had no idea how the Atlantic waves would toss and roll the ship. In the worst seas, the *Queen Mary* rolled 44 degrees.

NAMING A QUEEN

There are many stories about the *Queen Mary*, some true and some untrue. One of the untrue stories is that Cunard originally wanted to name their new liner the *Queen Victoria*. When the company approached King George V for his permission, they said that the new ship was to be named after the greatest queen in English history. The King said that his wife would be delighted. His wife, of course, was Queen Mary.

Everything that was not fixed to the floor followed. In one of the larger rooms, a piano broke free of its fixings, and crashed from side to side. It smashed against the costly furniture and panelling, emitting eerie twangs.

The ship's owners acted quickly. With the aid of carefully-positioned ballast (balancing weights) they made sure that the *Queen Mary* cut more smoothly through the waves. Soon the world's rich and famous queued to buy tickets.

Hairdressing and beauty parlours
These offered every service that you might expect in a beauty salon on land, including Vibro face massage and mudpacks. If you were curious, you could even have an X-ray (this was before the harmful effects of X-rays were realized).

Earplugs supplied
There were many musicians on board to entertain the passengers. So that they could practise without disturbing other passengers, there was a soundproofed studio with a piano.

Lift
There was a total of 21 lifts on board. They weren't just a luxury, because the ship was as tall as a 12-storey building. Moving supplies from deck to deck would have been very difficult without lifts.

Kennels
Dogs were luxuriously accommodated in 26 kennels. They even had their own 24-m exercise area — and a lamp-post.

Carpets
There were 9.6 km of carpets on board, all of them specially woven for the *Queen Mary*.

Bridge
High above the front decks was the bridge. From here the captain controlled the ship, and officers were on duty 24-hours a day to keep the ship on course. They also kept a lookout for icebergs — a frequent hazard in the North Atlantic.

Flowers
Hundreds of bunches of fresh flowers beautified the ship. They were all changed at the end of each trip. The *Queen Mary* had four gardeners.

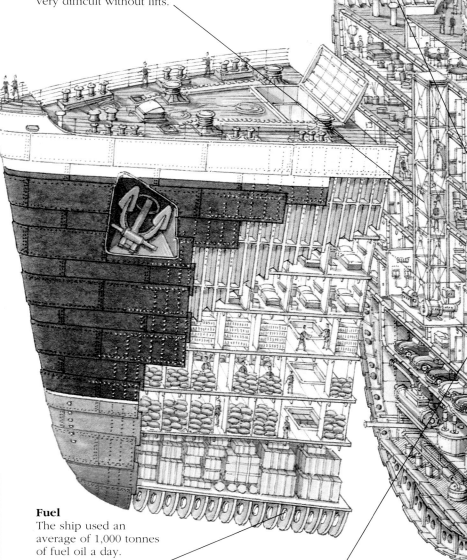

Fuel
The ship used an average of 1,000 tonnes of fuel oil a day.

Keel
The keel of the *Queen Mary* was made of huge plates 9 m long and 1.8 m deep, joined by riveted straps. The hull was plated with steel plates about 2.5 cm thick, and was either double- or triple-riveted.

Lighting
The 30,000 light bulbs on the ship required constant attention. A team of electricians spent half the night changing blown bulbs while the passengers were asleep.

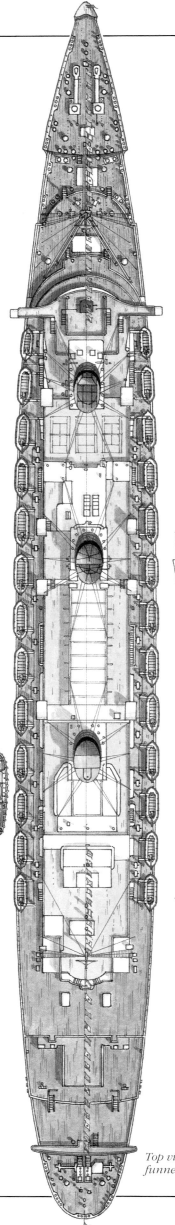

Top view showing funnels and decks

OCEAN LINER

When ocean travel was fast and fashionable, the world's great shipping lines battled for business just as airlines do today. In a bid to be fastest across the Atlantic, Britain's Cunard Line built the *Queen Mary*, at that time the largest passenger liner in history. The prize for a fast liner was "The Blue Riband (ribbon) of the Atlantic". This wasn't actually a ribbon at all, but an honorary title given to the ship that made the fastest crossing between the United States and Europe. The *Queen Mary* won the Blue Riband in August 1936 by crossing the ocean in just three minutes short of four days. A rival liner, the *Normandie*, regained the title the following year, but in August 1938 the *Queen Mary* once more took the honour, shaving two hours and 19 minutes off her previous record. The *Queen Mary* remained the fastest Atlantic passenger liner for 14 years and was used by film stars, politicians, and the rich and famous for crossing after crossing. The *Queen Mary* retired from passenger service in 1967 and is now permanently moored in California as a floating hotel and convention centre.

Side view showing superstructure

LENGTH

The size of the *Queen Mary* — longer than six Statues of Liberty — created vast problems for both the ship's builders and for the New York port authorities. Before the ship could be built, an enormous dry-dock had to be constructed in Britain. In New York, a special 305-metre pier was built.

LENGTH IN METRES

| 0 | 15 | 30 | 45 | 60 | 75 | 90 | 105 | 120 | 135 | 150 |

GULL'S EYE VIEW

Seen from above, the tiny tennis courts give a sense of the enormous scale of the *Queen Mary's* decks. Rigged in constant readiness, the lifeboats were capable of carrying 145 people each. Fortunately, they never had to be used.

THE ROUTE

The *Queen Mary* sailed between New York and Southampton, on Britain's south coast. The liner's owners built the ship to run a weekly service between the two ports. To make the crossing in less than five days and beat the record of other shipping lines, the *Queen Mary* had to average 28.5 knots (52.8 km/h).

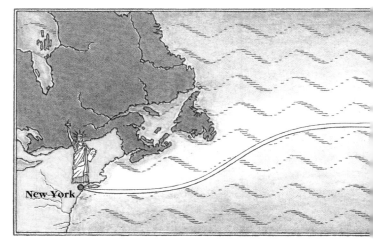

PROW AND PROPS

Sailing at 30 knots, the *Queen Mary's* white superstructure and red funnels made an awe-inspiring sight. 18,000 scale model tests ensured that the ship's towering bow (front) would cut cleanly through the water, powered forward by four 6-metre diameter propellers 300 metres to the rear at the stern (back) of the ship.

Bow view showing anchors and superstructure

Stern view showing rudder and propellers

DECKS AND CABINS

Careful planning enforced a strict social class system on board ship. The height above the waterline indicated status: passengers who paid the most for their tickets had airy views from the upper decks.

165   180   195   210   225   240   255   270   285   300

CUNARD

The Cunard Line was founded in 1839 by Samuel (later Sir Samuel) Cunard. Cunard started a transatlantic passenger service between Britain and the United States. Cunard's first ship was the *Britannia*, on which Charles Dickens, the British author, travelled to New York in 1842.

Southampton

THE HULL

Ten million rivets held together the 160 watertight compartments which divided up the vast hull. If the ship was holed, the water would fill only one compartment, and the ship would not sink. At the stern (rear) of the ship was the rudder, which was as big as a house and weighed 180 tonnes.

Bottom view showing propellers and keel

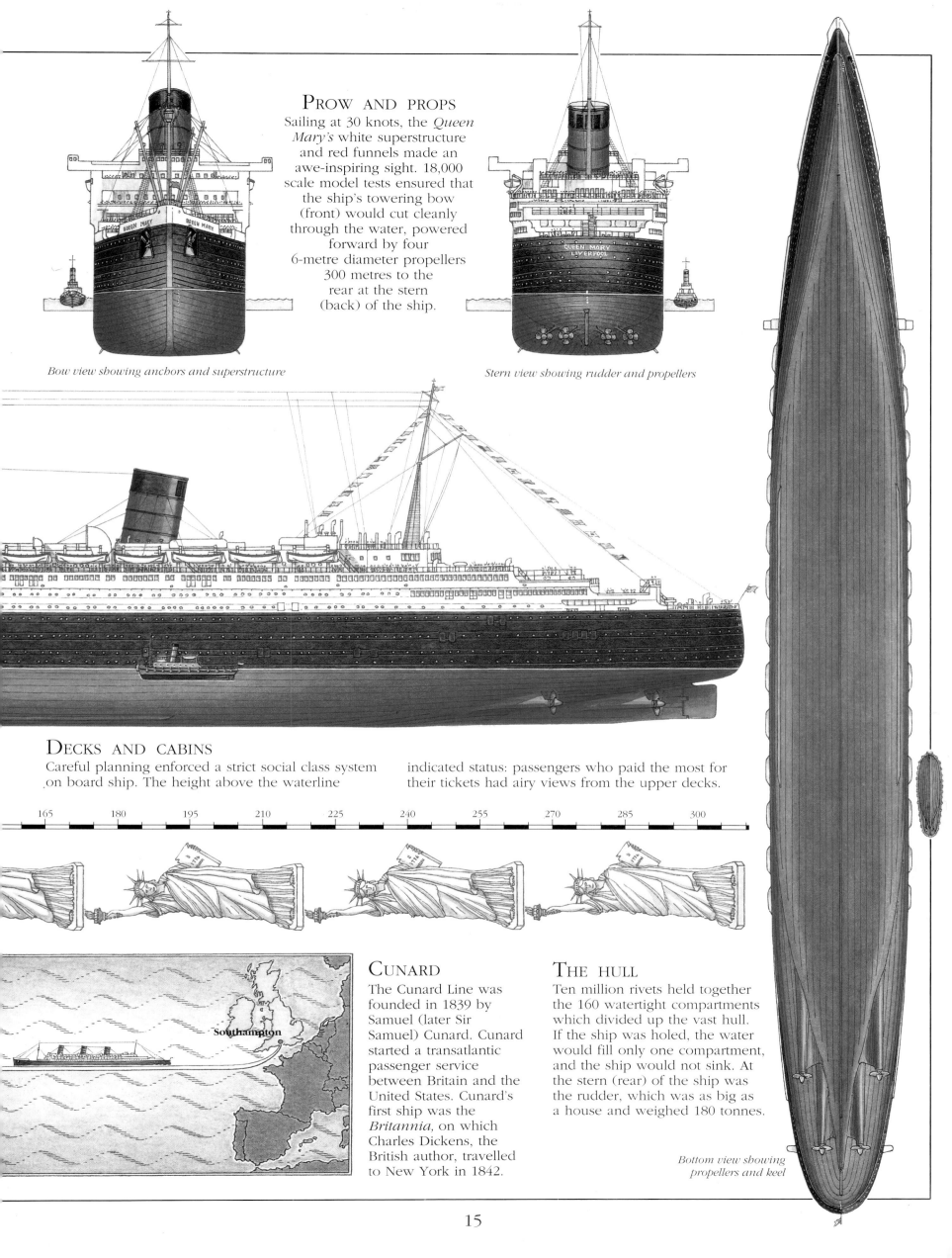

Length • 310.75 m	
Length at the waterline • 306 m	
Beam (width) • 36 m	
Draught (height underwater) • 11.83 m	
Speed • 28.5 knots	
Engine power • 212,000 horsepower	
Anchors • 4 x 16 tonnes, each with 600 m cable	

LIFE OF A ROYAL LADY

Construction work on the *Queen Mary* began in December 1930, but stopped during the Depression for more than two years. The liner was finally launched in 1934, and her maiden (first) voyage began on 27 May 1936. The ship was taken over by the Royal Navy in 1940 as a troop transport ship. The *Queen Mary* began carrying passengers again in 1947, and continued in service for another twenty years. But by 1967, air travel had made huge ocean liners obsolete, and the *Queen Mary* began her last voyage on 22 September.

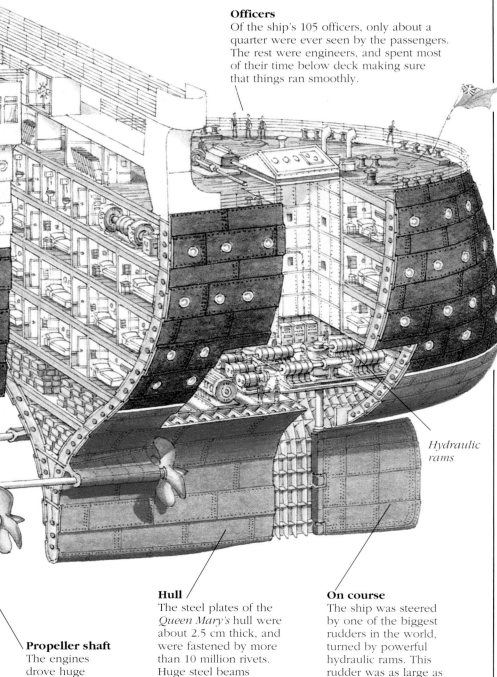

Officers
Of the ship's 105 officers, only about a quarter were ever seen by the passengers. The rest were engineers, and spent most of their time below deck making sure that things ran smoothly.

Hydraulic rams

Propeller shaft
The engines drove huge propeller shafts, each as wide as a tree-trunk.

Hull
The steel plates of the *Queen Mary's* hull were about 2.5 cm thick, and were fastened by more than 10 million rivets. Huge steel beams almost 30 cm thick held the ship together.

On course
The ship was steered by one of the biggest rudders in the world, turned by powerful hydraulic rams. This rudder was as large as a house and weighed as much as 18 ten-tonne trucks.

WHO WAS ON BOARD?

The *Queen Mary* could carry more than 1,400 passengers in three different classes – Cabin (First), Tourist (Second), and Third class. To keep all of them happy, the ship's crew included bell-boys, maids, nurses, and barmen – besides the engineers and quartermasters, stokers, and greasers needed simply to sail the ship.

THE CREW

Captain

25 Officers

80 Engineer Officers

200 Stewards and Leading seamen

100 Seamen and greasers

Chief steward

200 Stewardesses

200 Waiters

200 Cooks

50 Chefs

50 Nurses

Surgeon

Doctor

THE PASSENGERS

800 1st Class passengers

800 2nd Class passengers

600 3rd Class passengers

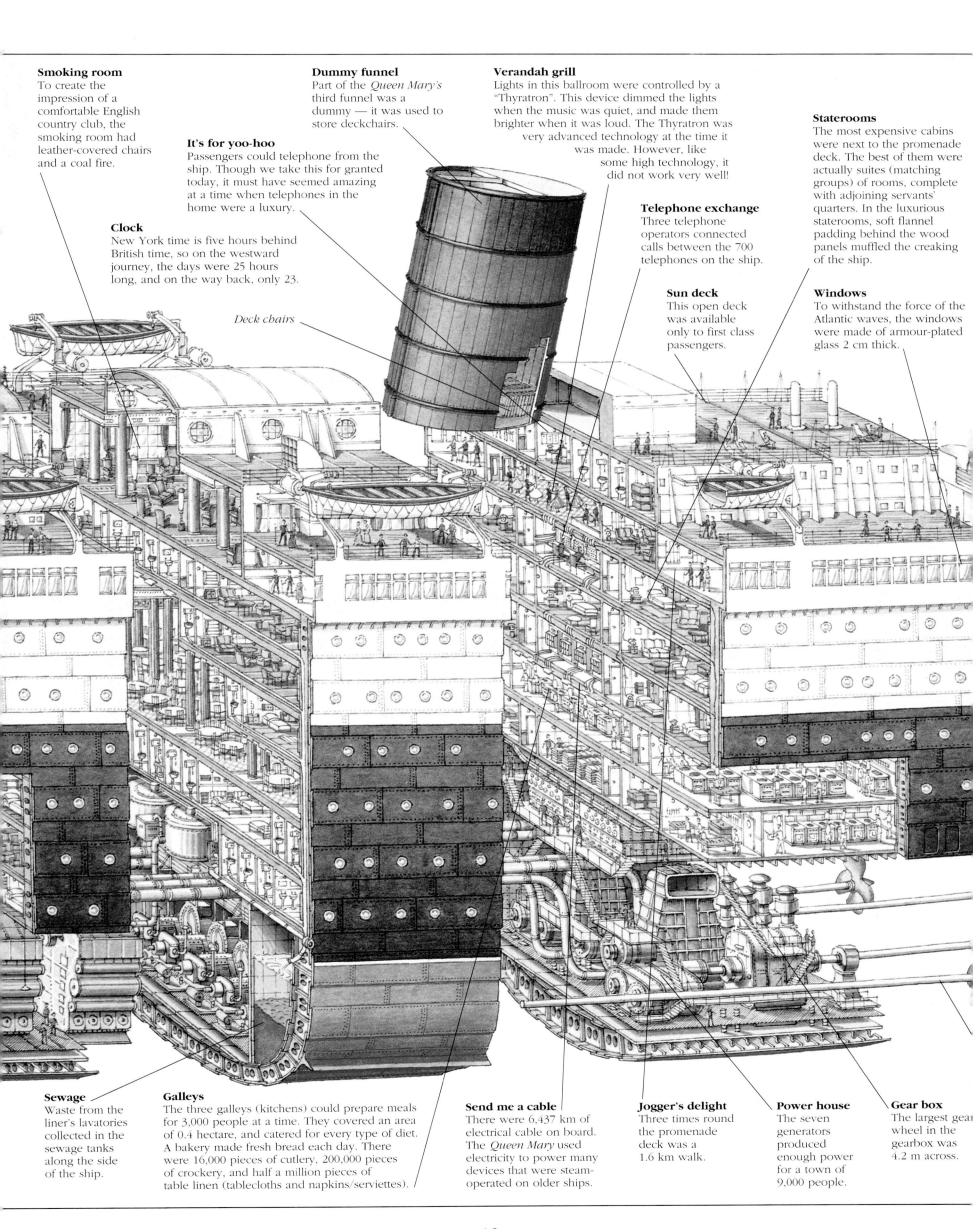

Smoking room
To create the impression of a comfortable English country club, the smoking room had leather-covered chairs and a coal fire.

Dummy funnel
Part of the *Queen Mary's* third funnel was a dummy — it was used to store deckchairs.

Verandah grill
Lights in this ballroom were controlled by a "Thyratron". This device dimmed the lights when the music was quiet, and made them brighter when it was loud. The Thyratron was very advanced technology at the time it was made. However, like some high technology, it did not work very well!

Staterooms
The most expensive cabins were next to the promenade deck. The best of them were actually suites (matching groups) of rooms, complete with adjoining servants' quarters. In the luxurious staterooms, soft flannel padding behind the wood panels muffled the creaking of the ship.

It's for yoo-hoo
Passengers could telephone from the ship. Though we take this for granted today, it must have seemed amazing at a time when telephones in the home were a luxury.

Clock
New York time is five hours behind British time, so on the westward journey, the days were 25 hours long, and on the way back, only 23.

Deck chairs

Telephone exchange
Three telephone operators connected calls between the 700 telephones on the ship.

Sun deck
This open deck was available only to first class passengers.

Windows
To withstand the force of the Atlantic waves, the windows were made of armour-plated glass 2 cm thick.

Sewage
Waste from the liner's lavatories collected in the sewage tanks along the side of the ship.

Galleys
The three galleys (kitchens) could prepare meals for 3,000 people at a time. They covered an area of 0.4 hectare, and catered for every type of diet. A bakery made fresh bread each day. There were 16,000 pieces of cutlery, 200,000 pieces of crockery, and half a million pieces of table linen (tablecloths and napkins/serviettes).

Send me a cable
There were 6,437 km of electrical cable on board. The *Queen Mary* used electricity to power many devices that were steam-operated on older ships.

Jogger's delight
Three times round the promenade deck was a 1.6 km walk.

Power house
The seven generators produced enough power for a town of 9,000 people.

Gear box
The largest gear wheel in the gearbox was 4.2 m across.

SUBMARINE

German submarines were among the most terrifying weapons of World War II (1939-45). Even now it is easy to see why. The submarines were invisible as they sneaked up on enemy shipping. When they got close enough to attack, they floated just below the surface. To aim weapons without coming to the surface, the submarine's commander used a periscope (a special telescope in a tube that poked up above the waves). When the target was directly ahead, the submarine launched a torpedo — a long, thin bomb powered by an electric motor. When it hit the target, the torpedo blew a hole in the ship, which quickly sank. The submarines and their crews nearly won the war for Germany. But Britain and the United States found new ways of detecting and destroying them, and by 1943 many of the German 'U-boats' (Underwater boats) had been sunk.

Radar antenna
This antenna detected aircraft radar, so that the U-boat could quickly dive to avoid attack.

Ouch!
In cold weather the crew could easily freeze to metal parts of the submarine. Wooden strips prevented this.

Magnetic compass
This type of compass had special compensation devices to make sure that it always pointed north.

Snorkel
The snorkel allowed the diesel engines to be used near the surface. It was a long tube that sucked air from the surface down into the submarine.

Is anybody there?
The commander used a simple tube to talk to the engine room.

Hatch
A powerful locking mechanism on the hatch made sure that no water leaked in when the submarine dived.

It's a bird...
A small periscope enabled the crew to search the sky for enemy planes.

Attack (main) periscope

Radio antenna

Air on tap
The submarine crew relied on compressed air to do many jobs: they breathed it; they launched torpedoes with it; they filled the diving tanks with it when they wanted to surface; and they even used compressed air to operate much of the ship's machinery.

Tidy torpedoes
Five torpedoes were kept ready to fire in their tubes. However, this exposed them to seawater, so each was removed from its tube and cleaned once a week.

Big bang
On the surface, the submarine could use its 8.8-cm gun to attack enemy shipping.

Anchor

Winch for moving torpedoes

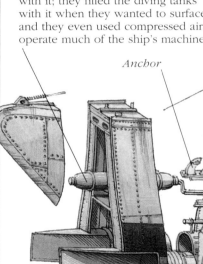

Torpedo tube

Flying underwater
When the submarine was moving underwater, the crew adjusted its depth using the hydroplanes. The hydroplanes were like short aircraft wings. They were operated by the two planesmen, and helped the submarine dive or surface. Angling them up made the submarine dive; angling them down made it surface.

Torpedoes in storage

That sinking feeling
The diving tank controlled the submarine's buoyancy — the level at which it floated in the water. When the submarine operated on the surface, the diving tanks were full of air. Releasing the air so that the tanks filled with water made the submarine dive deeper.

All change!
The crew worked in shifts — while some of them worked, the rest slept. There were only enough beds for one shift to sleep in at a time.

Submerged signals
The submarine could send and receive long wave radio signals even when the radio antenna was submerged in 9 m of water. All radio signals were in code, so that the enemy could not understand the messages if they intercepted them. The captain used a machine to code and decode incoming messages.

Base of attack periscope

Control room

Own goal
German submarines experimented with an acoustic torpedo. This steered towards its target by "listening" for the ship's engines. Some of the first experiments with acoustic torpedoes were disasters, because the submarine's engines were louder than those of the target; the torpedo turned round and blew up the submarine!

Look-out

Exhaust outlet

A lot of flak
The crew fired the flak gun at enemy aircraft.

Safety railings

Conning tower
The raised structure in the centre of the submarine was called the conning tower. The commander steered (or "conned") the submarine from here when the boat was running on the surface.

The wurst of it
Because of the lack of space, smoked meat, bread, and other supplies were stored anywhere there was room — in the crew's quarters, or even in the toilet!

Sub saddle
Large fuel tanks sat astride the submarine like a saddle on a horse's back.

U-BOAT TYPE VII-C

The German navy put 650 type VII-C U-boats into service during World War II. This submarine was cheaper to build and smaller than the submarines of Germany's enemies, but it had sufficient range to be able to carry out missions far out into the Atlantic Ocean. Although it was out-of-date by the end of the war, the VII-C was an advanced and dangerous weapon when it first appeared.

KEY FACTS	
Length • 67.1 m	
Maximum diameter • 6.18 m	
Surface range • 16,300 km at 18.5 km/h	
Submerged range • 147 km/7.4 km/h	
Maximum surface speed • 32 km/h	
Maximum submerged speed • 14 km/h	
Weapons • 14 torpedoes or up to 60 mines; 8.8-cm deck gun; anti-aircraft flak gun.	

Engine controls

Diesel engine silencers

Navigation light
On patrol, lights would have revealed the submarine's position to the enemy. So the lights were used only in friendly waters.

Torpedo tube

Rudders

Planesmen

Drive shaft to propeller

Torpedo

Rear hydroplanes

Propeller

Electric motor
When travelling underwater, the submarine was powered by electric motors. But long journeys underwater were impossible, because the batteries soon ran down, and had to be recharged.

Big batteries
The submarine carried enormous batteries to power the electric motor. They stored enough electricity to power 1,000 light bulbs for 24 hours.

Lockers
The crew's lockers were very small. One visitor described them as "the size of a briefcase".

Crude cooking
Cooking facilities were crude in the galley. The cook had just two hot plates.

Supply line
The amount of fuel the submarine could carry limited the range it could travel. To extend the range, the German navy built supply submarines — U-boats which carried only fuel and supplies.

Diesel power
Powerful diesel engines propelled the submarine forward on or near the surface. However, they could not be used deep underwater, because they needed air to operate. Starting the diesel engines while submerged would have rapidly sucked all the air out of the submarine, suffocating the crew.

COAL MINE

Inside a low tunnel 500 metres beneath our feet, coal miners operate machines that take great bites out of the Earth's crust, to extract coal from rock. In our bright homes above, many of us never see the coal that the miners and their machines dig out. Nevertheless we still use it: in every home, electricity generated by burning coal powers eight out of every ten light bulbs.

People began burning coal thousands of years ago. They probably began by using coal that they found on the surface of the ground. However, they soon began to dig pits and shafts to find coal seams — layers of coal buried in the rocks underground. In these early mines, miners daily risked their lives to dig out the "black gold" using pickaxes and shovels, and later explosives. Today's miners are helped by computers and giant diggers, but mines are still dark, damp, dirty, and dangerous places.

Powered roof supports

Shearer loader

Road heading machine

The modern mine relies on machinery, not muscle power, to extract coal. The vicious-looking **road heading machine** uses its spinning bit to drill out the roads to the coal face (the part of the mine where coal is actually being dug out). The **shearer loader** moves across the coal face tearing through coal and rock with diamond-tipped blades attached to a rotating drum. **Powered roof supports** hold up the roof as the shearer loader advances. The supports also push the conveyor which carries coal away from the face.

Pit head
Most of the mine is below ground but work also takes place on the surface. The offices and workshops above ground are called the pit head.

Back to nature
A vast amount of work is being undertaken to restore the sites of old collieries and return them to nature.

Sorting shafts

Winding gear
Powerful winches at the top of the shaft raise skips of coal to the surface, and lower miners down the shaft in a cage — a kind of lift.

Store
In the pithead buildings there are stores, and workshops where apparatus needed in the mine can be assembled.

Recreation hall

Car park

Ventilation shaft

Fan housing

Fan house
Huge fans suck stale air out of the mine and draw fresh air in.

Moving underground
Mines use many different sorts of transport. In the larger roads electric or diesel locomotives haul trains. Free Steered Vehicles (FSVs) are diesel powered tractor units which also move miners and equipment.

Fan blades

Upcast shaft
Every mine has at least two shafts. Stale air is drawn out of the mine through the upcast shaft.

Conveyor

Coal separators

Lift to transport miners to coal face

Cleaning and grading
Coal that comes out of the mine is mixed with a lot of mud and rock. Before the lumps of coal can be sold they must be cleaned and graded — sorted into different qualities and sizes. Tanks of water separate coal from rock: the coal floats, but the rock sinks.

Landscaping
In the past, mining was not attractive, but modern pits have been designed to blend with the landscape to minimize the impact on surroundings.

Moving coal
Coal is rarely mined where it is needed, so trains and heavy lorries carry it away from the mine.

Finding coal
Coal is found underground in thin layers called seams. Some coal seams are up to 6 m thick; but seams as thin as 200 cm may still contain enough coal to be worthwhile mining.

Showers
At the pit head the miners can have showers and a meal. Everyone has a locker to store their working clothes when they go home.

Canteen

Bright idea
To see in the darkness of the pit, every miner has a battery-powered lamp. The lamp is strapped to a helmet, so that the miner's hands are free. The miners recharge the batteries of their lamps in the lamp room.

Tunnel supports

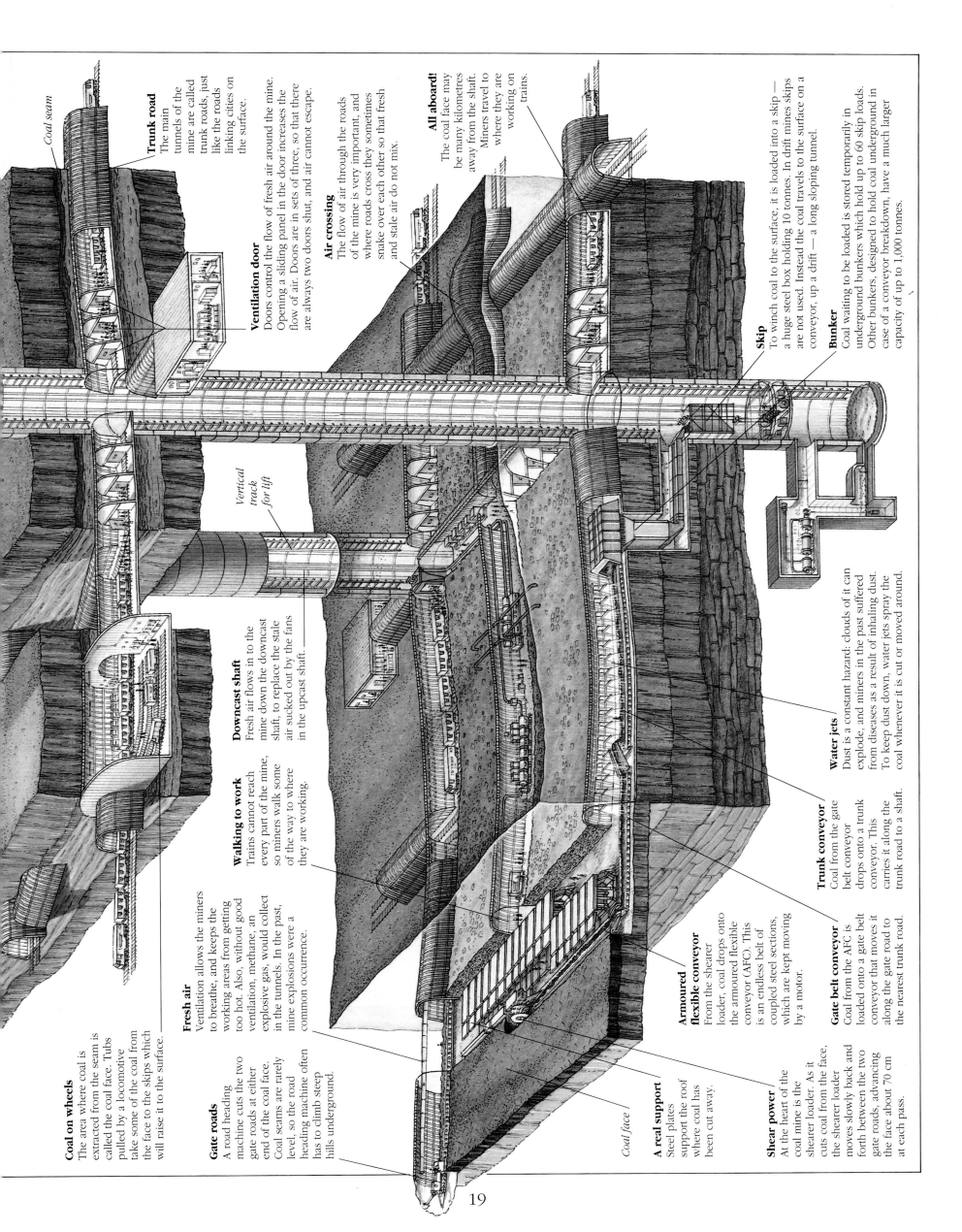

Coal seam

Trunk road
The main tunnels of the mine are called trunk roads, just like the roads linking cities on the surface.

Ventilation door
Doors control the flow of fresh air around the mine. Opening a sliding panel in the door increases the flow of air. Doors are in sets of three, so that fresh air cannot escape. There are always two doors shut, and air cannot escape.

Air crossing
The flow of air through the roads of the mine is very important, and where roads cross they sometimes snake over each other so that fresh and stale air do not mix.

All aboard!
The coal face may be many kilometres away from the shaft. Miners travel to where they are working on trains.

Skip
To winch coal to the surface, it is loaded into a skip — a huge steel box holding 10 tonnes. In drift mines skips are not used. Instead the coal travels to the surface on a conveyor, up a drift — a long sloping tunnel.

Bunker
Coal waiting to be loaded is stored temporarily in underground bunkers which hold up to 60 skip loads. Other bunkers, designed to hold coal underground in case of a conveyor breakdown, have a much larger capacity of up to 1,000 tonnes.

Vertical track for lift

Downcast shaft
Fresh air flows in to the mine down the downcast shaft, to replace the stale air sucked out by the fans in the upcast shaft.

Walking to work
Trains cannot reach every part of the mine, so miners walk some of the way to where they are working.

Trunk conveyor
Coal from the gate belt conveyor drops onto a trunk conveyor. This carries it along the trunk road to a shaft.

Water jets
Dust is a constant hazard: clouds of it can explode, and miners in the past suffered from diseases as a result of inhaling dust. To keep dust down, water jets spray the coal whenever it is cut or moved around.

Coal on wheels
The area where coal is extracted from the seam is called the coal face. Tubs pulled by a locomotive take some of the coal from the face to the skips which will raise it to the surface.

Gate roads
A road heading machine cuts the two gate roads at either end of the coal face. Coal seams are rarely level, so the road heading machine often has to climb steep hills underground.

Fresh air
Ventilation allows the miners to breathe, and keeps the working areas from getting too hot. Also, without good ventilation, methane, an explosive gas, would collect in the tunnels. In the past, mine explosions were a common occurrence.

Shear power
At the heart of the coal mine is the shearer loader. As it cuts coal from the face, the shearer loader moves slowly back and forth between the two gate roads, advancing the face about 70 cm at each pass.

A real support
Steel plates support the roof where coal has been cut away.

Gate belt conveyor
Coal from the AFC is loaded onto a gate belt conveyor that moves it along the gate road to the nearest trunk road.

Armoured flexible conveyor
From the shearer loader, coal drops onto the armoured flexible conveyor (AFC). This is an endless belt of coupled steel sections, which are kept moving by a motor.

Coal face

19

TANK

Five hundred years ago, the Italian artist and inventor Leonardo da Vinci (1452-1519) dreamed up terrible fighting machines. They could cross muddy battlefields with ease, and metal armour protected them from attack. By the start of World War II in 1939, European armies were equipped with large numbers of tanks, all formidable fighting machines, equipped with linked steel caterpillar tracks so that they could cross any terrain, in any weather.

Fighting in a tank such as the Soviet T-34 shown here was a horrible job. The inside of the tank was incredibly cramped, noisy, and uncomfortable. Ammunition and fuel enclosed the crew on all sides, so a direct hit from an enemy shell usually made the tank explode or catch fire. But despite the danger, tanks proved to be very successful.

Big shot
The tank's gun was a formidable weapon. It could fire high-explosive, armour-piercing or shrapnel shells. The armour-piercing shells could penetrate 65 mm of armour plating.

Rifling
Grooves in the barrel made the shells spin and follow a straight path.

What did you say?
Until 1943 few tanks had radios. Crews had to use signal flags to send messages to other tanks.

Deadly drums
The tank had two machine guns, both of which used ammunition in drums holding 63 rounds each. A bag collected the spent cartridge cases.

Air cylinders
The tank had an electric starter motor, but if this failed the crew could start the engine using compressed air from cylinders at the front of the tank.

Accelerator

Driver
The driver controlled the tank using two steering levers, each of which started or stopped one of the two tracks to turn the tank.

Brake

Clutch

Foot firing
The gunner/commander used pedals to fire the main gun and one of the machine guns. The loader could also fire both guns with hand triggers.

Shell collection
Shells were hard to reach. They were mainly stored in bins under the gunner's feet. In battle the turret quickly became strewn with open ammunition bins.

Elevation control
Turning the elevation wheel raised or lowered the gun. The control was hard to operate, and if the gunner had long legs, the wheel banged his knees when he turned it.

Wireless aerial

Dual role
This tank had a crew of only four (most tanks have crews of five or more) so the commander also had to act as gunner. In practice he was overworked and did neither job well.

Loader
The loader had an uncomfortable job. The ammunition bin lids were hard to get off, and the cramped turret made it difficult to lift the 9.5 kg shells to the breech of the gun.

Hinge

In the sights
The gunner/commander aimed the gun using one of two sights. One provided a view through a periscope on the turret roof. The other gun-sight was a telescope pointing directly forward.

Guide-horn
A guide-horn on alternate links kept the links engaged with the tank's wheels.

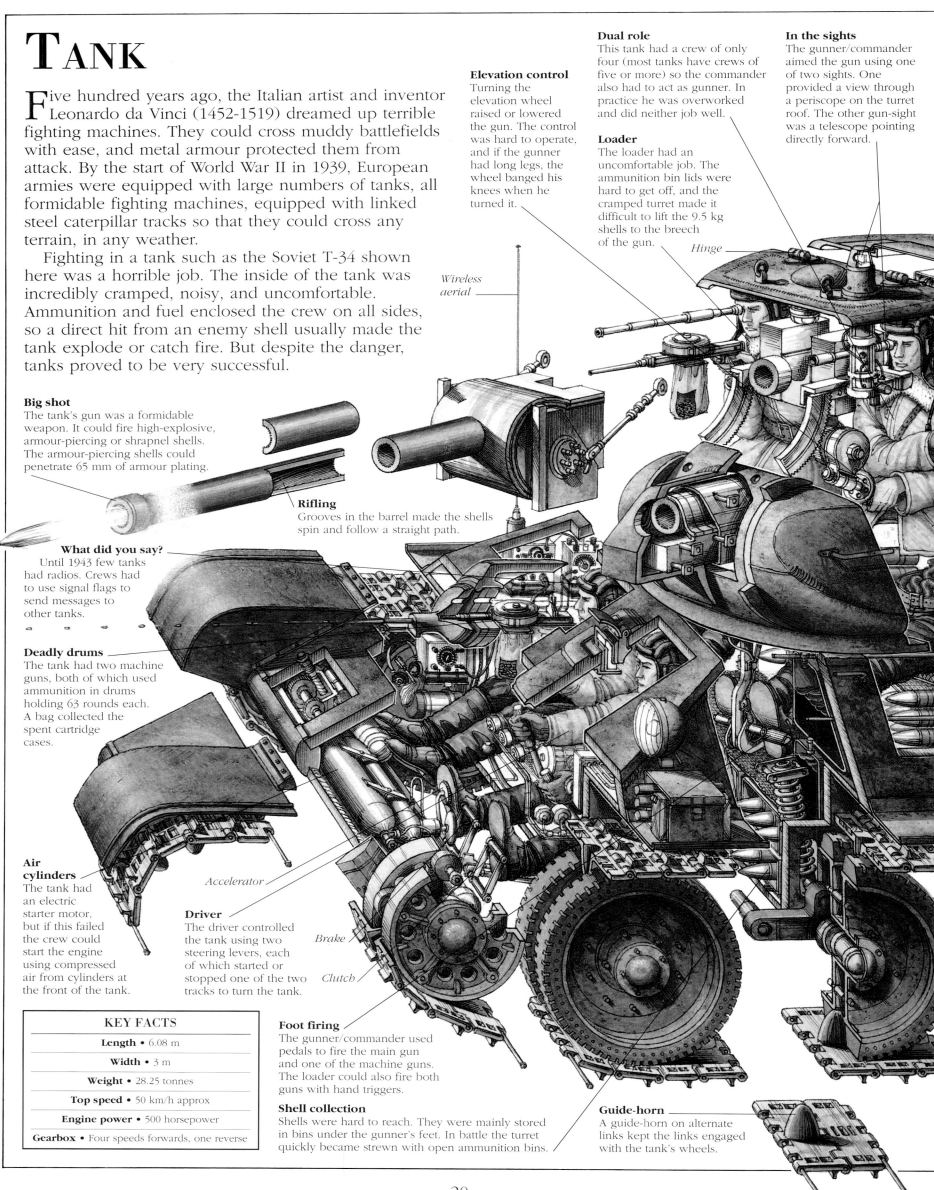

KEY FACTS	
Length • 6.08 m	
Width • 3 m	
Weight • 28.25 tonnes	
Top speed • 50 km/h approx	
Engine power • 500 horsepower	
Gearbox • Four speeds forwards, one reverse	

Design flaw
The turret hatch opened forwards, but when open it blocked the view of the way ahead. Consequently, Soviet tank commanders could not observe the battle from the open hatch without exposing themselves to enemy fire.

Tough turret
The T-34's turret housed the large gun and could rotate right around. It was made of very hard steel armour plate.

Electric traverse motor

Crude construction
T-34 tanks were crudely made compared to their German and British counterparts. Soviet engineering was primitive and resources scarce, so the factories carefully ground and polished only where absolutely necessary. However, the rough finish did not reduce the tank's effectiveness.

All the way round
There was a motor to traverse, or rotate, the turret, and the gunner could also use a hand-wheel for traversing. However, the hand-wheel was in an awkward position, and the gunner had to reach across and turn it with his right hand.

Narrow view
The gunner/commander could see the battlefield through a periscope, but this provided a very narrow field of view.

Last resort
If the tank crew ran out of shells and ammunition for their machine guns, they defended themselves by firing hand-guns through these tiny ports.

Turret seats
The turret crew sat on seats attached to the turret itself. When the turret turned, they turned with it.

Fuel tank

Plenty of power
The tank's 39-litre V-12 engine generated 500 horsepower. It was capable of propelling the tank at speeds of up to 50 km/h on a good road.

DEADLY WEAPON

When the Soviet T-34 tank first appeared in 1941 it was without doubt the best-designed tank in the world. It was highly mobile, had a powerful gun, and very solid armour. Unfortunately the tanks were manufactured in a great hurry, so that some parts were crudely made and of poor quality. In addition, Soviet tank crews often only received 72 hours training before going into action.

Engine air filter

Engine covering

Exhaust pipe

Engine cooling fan

What no lav!
You'll notice that there are no "facilities" on board the tank. The crew either left the tank or used an empty shell case to answer a call of nature.

Gearbox
The tank's gearbox was very easy to reach for maintenance. This was fortunate, since early models had serious defects. Gearbox problems immobilised more tanks in 1941 than enemy action.

Amazing armour
The high quality of the T-34 armour plating meant that the tank could withstand attack better than the German Pz Kpfw III tanks that it met in battle. The armour was 45 mm thick on the turret front, but in later models this was increased to 65 mm.

Towing cables

Gripping grousers
Bolt-on plates, called grousers, provided extra grip in mud or snow.

Wheels
Owing to a shortage of rubber in 1942, T-34 tanks began to be made with solid metal wheels. However, this caused terrible vibration which shook parts loose. The problem was solved by putting rubber treads on the first and fifth wheels.

Suspension
The tank's suspension gave a comfortable ride, but made it difficult to aim the gun accurately while the tank was moving. Modern tanks solve this problem by using devices to stabilise the gun.

Making tracks
The manganese steel tracks spread the enormous weight of the tank, so that it did not sink into the mud of the battlefield. Ground pressure beneath the track was very low — only about double the pressure under a human foot, and less than half the pressure under a car tyre.

OIL RIG

Filling the fuel tank of a car couldn't be simpler. But extracting oil from which to make the petrol is very difficult indeed. To understand the challenge of drilling for oil, think about standing at the top of a two-metre step ladder. Most of the ladder is under water. Now drill a hole the width of a pencil in the ground beneath the ladder. You need a very long drill, because the hole is 30 metres deep.

Sounds difficult? Drilling for oil at sea is much harder. Much of the world's oil is buried under the sea. Giant oil production platforms may be more than 215 metres high, but only a quarter shows above the waves. The rest is a strong frame anchored to the sea bed. The platform supports the rig — the apparatus that drills down to the oil, as well as storage tanks, pumps, and living quarters for the workers, who live on the rig for two weeks at a time.

DRILLING FOR OIL

The part of the platform that drills down to reach the oil reserves is called the rig. The rig's motor turns a rotary table, which then turns a long shaft, called the drill string, which has a drill bit on the end. The drill bit has hard teeth which cut through the rock below. As the shaft gets deeper, the drillers add on 9-metre long pieces of pipe. The most visible part of the entire oil platform, called the derrick, is 60 metres high and supports the winch and crane which hold up the drill string. The drill string may weigh hundreds of tonnes, and the crane must be powerful enough to pull the entire string from the shaft.

As drilling progresses, a mix of chemicals called mud is pumped down the drill string to keep the drill bit cool and bring rocks to the surface. The mud then carries the mud back to the platform. The mud is filtered, and pumped back down the drill string.

When a drill strikes oil, the shaft becomes a producing well. An arrangement of valves called a Christmas tree is fitted to the top of the shaft, and regulates the flow of oil from the well. A single production platform may have as many as 30-40 wells.

If a drill bit strikes oil or gas under pressure, there can be a blow-out — oil or gas rushes up the drill pipe, and gushes out. A device called a blow-out preventer guards against this.

Around the clock
Kitchens on the rig stay open day and night. Oil production is continuous, and there are people working all the time.

Accommodation block
More than 100 workers live on the rig. It is home for two weeks at a time, so everything they need for work and recreation is supplied.

Loading bay
A crane unloads supplies from a small ship when the weather is calm enough for the ship to safely sail close to the platform.

Helicopter landing pad
Workers and supplies arrive by helicopter. In very bad weather ships cannot reach the platform, and the helicopter is the only link to the mainland.

Gas
Most wells produce gas as well as oil. Gas is used in the platform's power plant. Excess gas is burnt off at the rig's flare stack.

Control room
All the operations of the platform can be monitored and managed from here. Computers help control the flow of gas and oil.

Cinema
Boredom is a big problem for offshore workers, but a cinema breaks up the monotony.

Power station
The platform uses electricity for powering systems such as heating and lighting and also for pumping gas and oil ashore.

Roughnecks
The team of workers who operate the drilling rig are called roughnecks.

Lifeboat
This lifeboat can be lowered into the water. Other types of lifeboat slide down ramps for a quick escape.

Firm support
Strong steel girders support the decks of the platform.

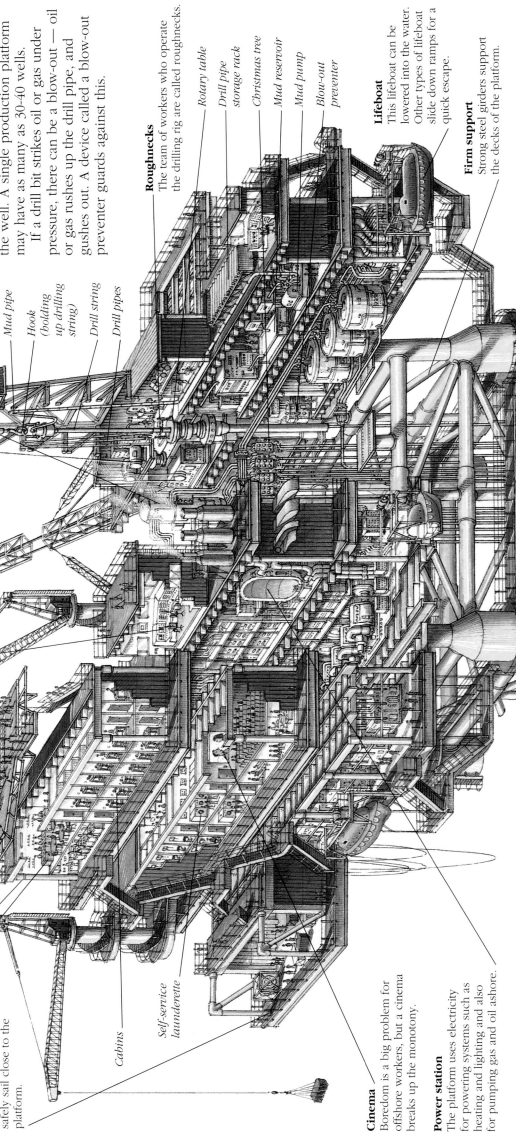

Derrick

Mud pipe

Hook (holding up drilling string)

Drill string

Drill pipes

Winch

Flare stack

Self-service launderette

Cabins

Rotary table

Drill pipe storage rack

Christmas tree

Mud reservoir

Mud pump

Blow-out preventer

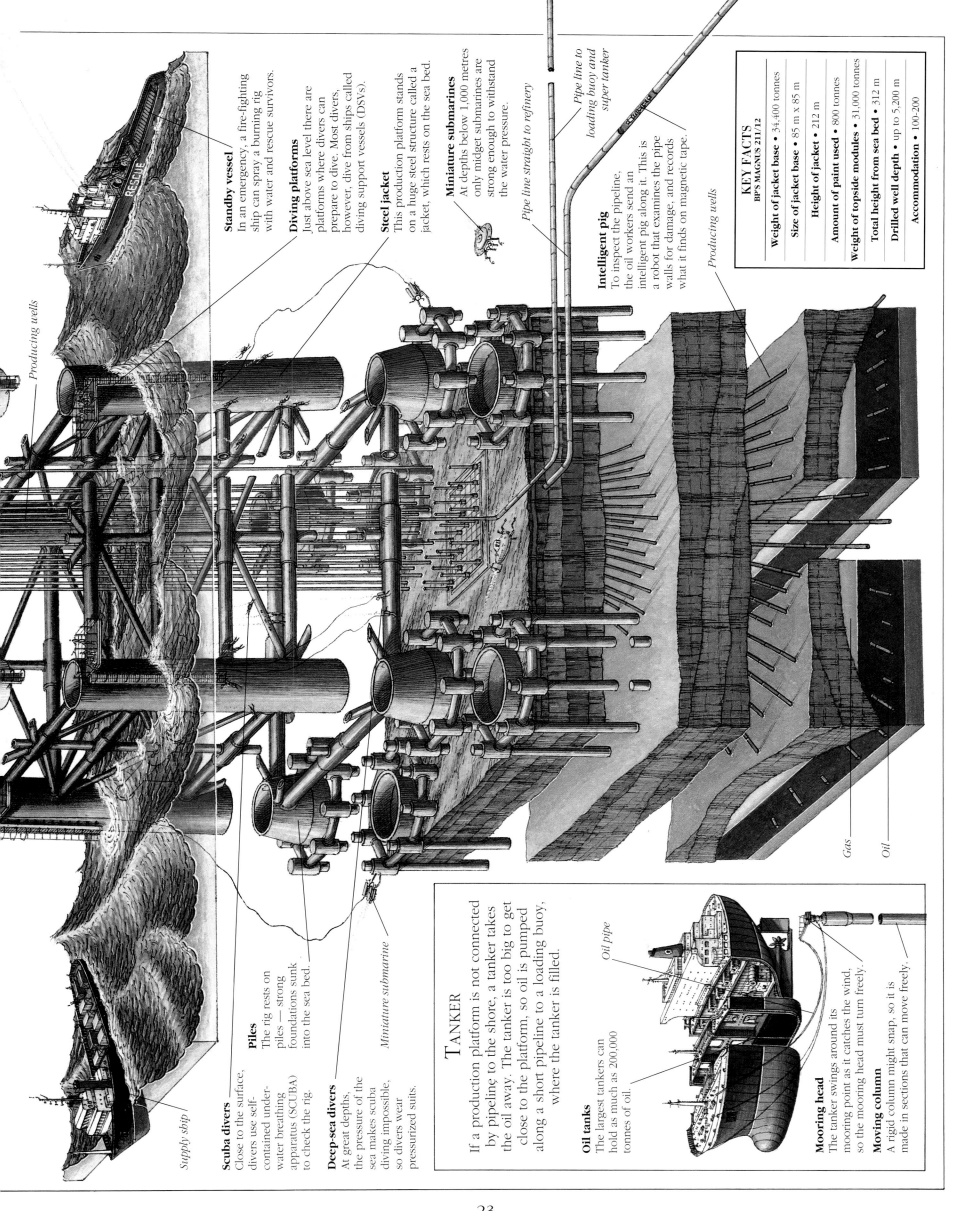

Producing wells

Supply ship

Standby vessel
In an emergency, a fire-fighting ship can spray a burning rig with water and rescue survivors.

Diving platforms
Just above sea level there are platforms where divers can prepare to dive. Most divers, however, dive from ships called diving support vessels (DSVs).

Steel jacket
This production platform stands on a huge steel structure called a jacket, which rests on the sea bed.

Scuba divers
Close to the surface, divers use self-contained underwater breathing apparatus (SCUBA) to check the rig.

Piles
The rig rests on piles — strong foundations sunk into the sea bed.

Deep-sea divers
At great depths, the pressure of the sea makes scuba diving impossible, so divers wear pressurized suits.

Miniature submarine

Miniature submarines
At depths below 1,000 metres only midget submarines are strong enough to withstand the water pressure.

Pipe line straight to refinery

Pipe line to loading buoy and super tanker

Intelligent pig
To inspect the pipeline, the oil workers send an intelligent pig along it. This is a robot that examines the pipe walls for damage, and records what it finds on magnetic tape.

Producing wells

Gas

Oil

TANKER

If a production platform is not connected by pipeline to the shore, a tanker takes the oil away. The tanker is too big to get close to the platform, so oil is pumped along a short pipeline to a loading buoy, where the tanker is filled.

Oil pipe

Oil tanks
The largest tankers can hold as much as 200,000 tonnes of oil.

Mooring head
The tanker swings around its mooring point as it catches the wind, so the mooring head must turn freely.

Moving column
A rigid column might snap, so it is made in sections that can move freely.

CATHEDRAL

Soaring high over the city skyline, the spires and roofs of a cathedral are a breathtaking sight. Cathedrals are just as amazing inside. They astonish the visitor with stained glass, and with beautiful stone and wood carved into intricate shapes and patterns. Creating a cathedral today would be an enormous and expensive task. And when most European cathedrals were built centuries ago, everything in them had to be laboriously carved by hand. Cathedral builders were not thinking about modern tourists when they began their work. They were building a place of prayer and worship, for the glory of God.

Today cathedrals still play an important part in the Christian religion. Each is the special central church of a diocese (religious district). The bishop of the diocese leads the worship in the cathedral.

JEWEL OF FRANCE

The cathedral cross-section on these pages is based on the famous cathedral at Chartres, France. This was built between the years 1195-1260 and is considered by many experts to be the most perfect of Europe's cathedrals. The original builders of Chartres envisioned the completed structure with nine towers, but only two were completed.

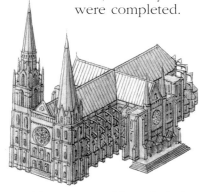

This is a view of the cathedral as it stands today.

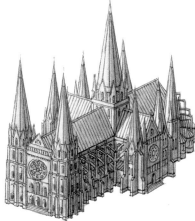

The original plan of the cathedral had nine towers, including a massive central spire.

Bells
Bells were installed in the tower of the cathedral to call people to worship. The biggest often weighed more than one tonne. A group of bells with different notes is called a peal. They can be rung in thousands of different combinations.

Spitting water
Rainwater spouted from the roof through the mouths of grotesque stone figures called gargoyles.

Flying buttresses
The cathedral's builders used buttresses to support the weight of the roof. These are great stone columns built on the outside of the cathedral. They carry the weight down to the ground. Flying buttresses have arches which hold up the upper parts of the walls.

Triforium
Halfway up the wall of the cathedral is the triforium: an arched passageway.

Niches
On the front of the cathedral there are many statues, each in a niche (an individual alcove). Today, most of the statues are just plain stone-coloured, but they were once painted in bright hues.

Main entrance
Most people enter the cathedral through a door in the west front.

Buttress

Nave
The people who come to worship in the cathedral enter the nave, the main body of the cathedral. Today there are usually pews (seats) here, but for many centuries the nave was an open area where worshippers stood.

Staircase
Climbing a lot of stairs is the only way to reach the roof, and this partly explains why fire destroyed so many cathedrals. To put out the flames, people passed buckets of water from hand to hand. Much of the water slopped out by the time the buckets reached the fire.

Maze
Many medieval (A.D. 800-1450) cathedrals had mazes built into the floors. A walk along the maze probably represented a pilgrimage (holy journey) to Jerusalem in the Holy Land (now in Israel).

Crypt
Underneath much of the cathedral is a crypt — a kind of cellar. Often the crypt is a burial place for officials of the church and other important people.

Organ
Music has been important in Christian worship for centuries. Organs were first used in European cathedrals more than a thousand years ago.

Roof beams
The cathedral roof is a network of huge timbers, and thin strips of wood. A thin skin of lead or copper makes the roof waterproof.

Stained glass
Stained glass windows held thousands of pieces of coloured glass. Each window told a Bible story in pictures.

Brick vaulting (curved ceilings)

Choir
The part of the cathedral where the choir stand to sing is also called the choir. The choir and altar were separated from the rest of the church by a partition called a rood screen.

MEET THE TEAM

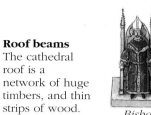
Bishop

Priests & Canons

Pilgrim

Master Mason

Cutter   Plumber   Sawyer   Carpenter

Woodman   Setter   Glazier   Smith   Labourer

The **bishop** was the leader of worship in the cathedral. He had help in organising worship from **priests** and **canons**, and possibly from monks if the cathedral was attached to a monastery.

The **master mason**, who designed the structure, led the building team. **Cutters** shaped the stone, and **setters** put it in place. **Sawyers** cut timber, and **carpenters** made all the wooden parts of the cathedral, including the scaffolding the others worked from. **Smiths** made the metal fittings, and **glaziers** the beautiful windows.

Presbytery
The bishop and priests traditionally lead worship in the cathedral from the presbytery, an area at the eastern end containing the altar.

Altar
The altar itself is the most important place in the cathedral. It was placed according to where the sun rose on the saint's day of the cathedral. For instance, St Patrick's day is on 17 March, so in a cathedral dedicated to (named for) St Patrick, the altar was aligned with the sunrise on 17 March.

Shaping the arches
To make sure that all the pieces of stone fitted together, the masons used templates. These were wooden patterns, made to exactly life size. As they carved the stone, the masons held the templates against the stonework, to make sure they didn't chip too much away.

Apse
The eastern end of the cathedral, called the apse, is often semi-circular in shape. The altar is at the centre of the apse.

Lady chapel
Many cathedrals have chapels dedicated to the Virgin Mary, Jesus Christ's mother. The chapel is called the "Lady Chapel" because Mary is also called "Our Lady".

Ambulatory
Surrounding the apse is an ambulatory, or walkway.

Chantry chapel
Wealthy supporters of the cathedral often gave money to have a chapel built in their memory when they died. They also paid for a priest to say Mass there, because they thought that this would help them get to heaven.

Solid foundations
Every cathedral needed lots of stone in its construction. Strong foundations supported the huge weight of the building above.

Chip off the old block
Much of the cathedral was prefabricated: masons carved the stonework roughly to shape at the quarry, and finished it off on the building site.

Transept
The transepts cross the nave. They make the plan of the cathedral into a cross shape, to remind Christians of the wooden cross on which Christ was nailed.

Throngs of people
Enormous numbers of tourists visit Europe's great cathedrals to wonder at the beautiful craftsmanship. Some may even pause and pray. In the past, cathedrals were just as crowded, but with pilgrims — people who travelled to cathedrals for prayer and worship.

Shrine
Cathedrals often had shrines. These were chambers containing relics — objects of special religious importance, such as the bones of a saint, or a piece of Christ's cross. Many people visited cathedrals to worship at shrines.

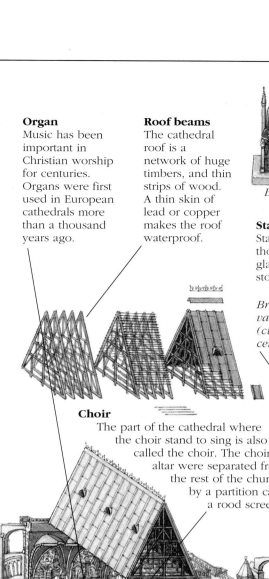
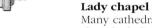

JUMBO JET

Imagine a small town and all its people suddenly plucked from the ground, and flying through the air at hundreds of kilometres an hour. Imagine this flying town has power, heating, and sewerage plants, and carries enough food and drink to keep everyone well-fed for a day. Now imagine hundreds of such towns flying high above tall mountains, deep oceans, and polar icecaps. They carry their human cargo to a strict timetable, in greater safety than a car. But

this flying town is not imaginary. It is a Boeing 747 aeroplane, or jumbo jet. The 747 is the world's largest passenger aeroplane, and it can carry 400 people. The 747 began service in 1969. The aircraft shown here was one of the first — PanAm's N732. Since then, 747s have flown a billion people more than 24 billion kilometres — that's like flying everybody on the Earth to the Moon and back 6,000 times.

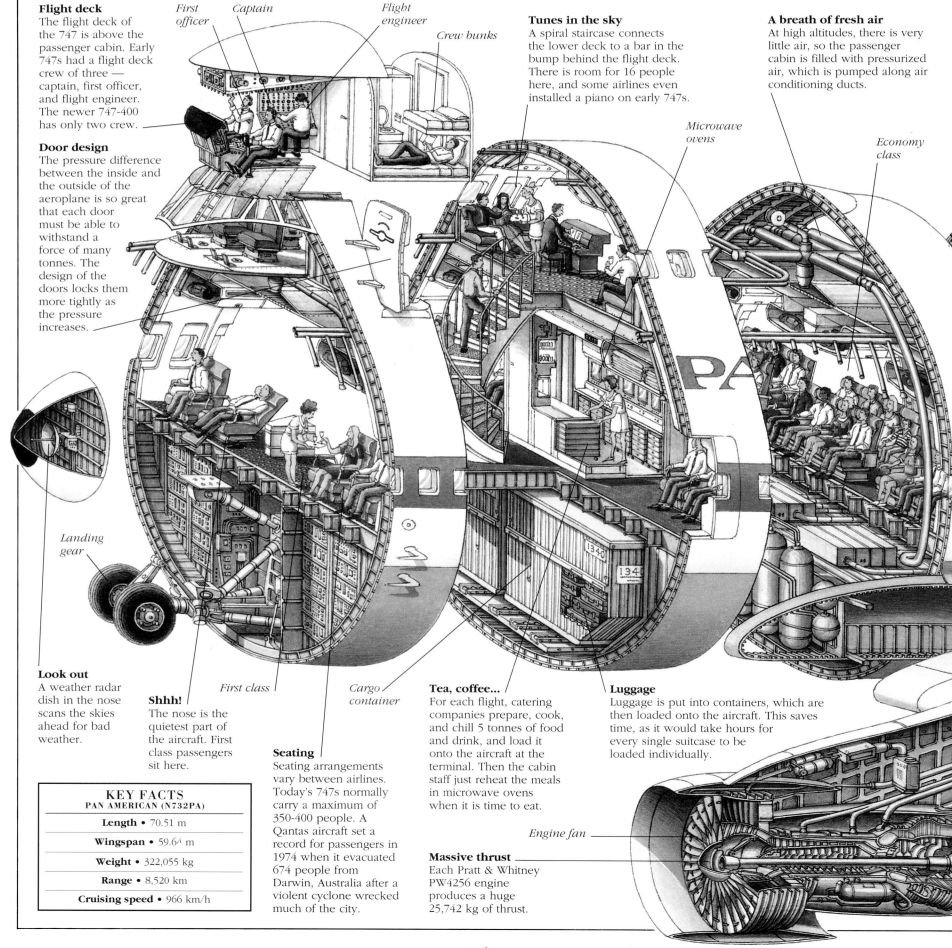

Flight deck
The flight deck of the 747 is above the passenger cabin. Early 747s had a flight deck crew of three — captain, first officer, and flight engineer. The newer 747-400 has only two crew.

First officer *Captain* *Flight engineer* *Crew bunks*

Door design
The pressure difference between the inside and the outside of the aeroplane is so great that each door must be able to withstand a force of many tonnes. The design of the doors locks them more tightly as the pressure increases.

Tunes in the sky
A spiral staircase connects the lower deck to a bar in the bump behind the flight deck. There is room for 16 people here, and some airlines even installed a piano on early 747s.

A breath of fresh air
At high altitudes, there is very little air, so the passenger cabin is filled with pressurized air, which is pumped along air conditioning ducts.

Microwave ovens

Economy class

Landing gear

Look out
A weather radar dish in the nose scans the skies ahead for bad weather.

First class

Shhh!
The nose is the quietest part of the aircraft. First class passengers sit here.

Cargo container

Seating
Seating arrangements vary between airlines. Today's 747s normally carry a maximum of 350-400 people. A Qantas aircraft set a record for passengers in 1974 when it evacuated 674 people from Darwin, Australia after a violent cyclone wrecked much of the city.

Tea, coffee...
For each flight, catering companies prepare, cook, and chill 5 tonnes of food and drink, and load it onto the aircraft at the terminal. Then the cabin staff just reheat the meals in microwave ovens when it is time to eat.

Luggage
Luggage is put into containers, which are then loaded onto the aircraft. This saves time, as it would take hours for every single suitcase to be loaded individually.

Engine fan

Massive thrust
Each Pratt & Whitney PW4256 engine produces a huge 25,742 kg of thrust.

KEY FACTS
PAN AMERICAN (N732PA)
Length • 70.51 m
Wingspan • 59.64 m
Weight • 322,055 kg
Range • 8,520 km
Cruising speed • 966 km/h

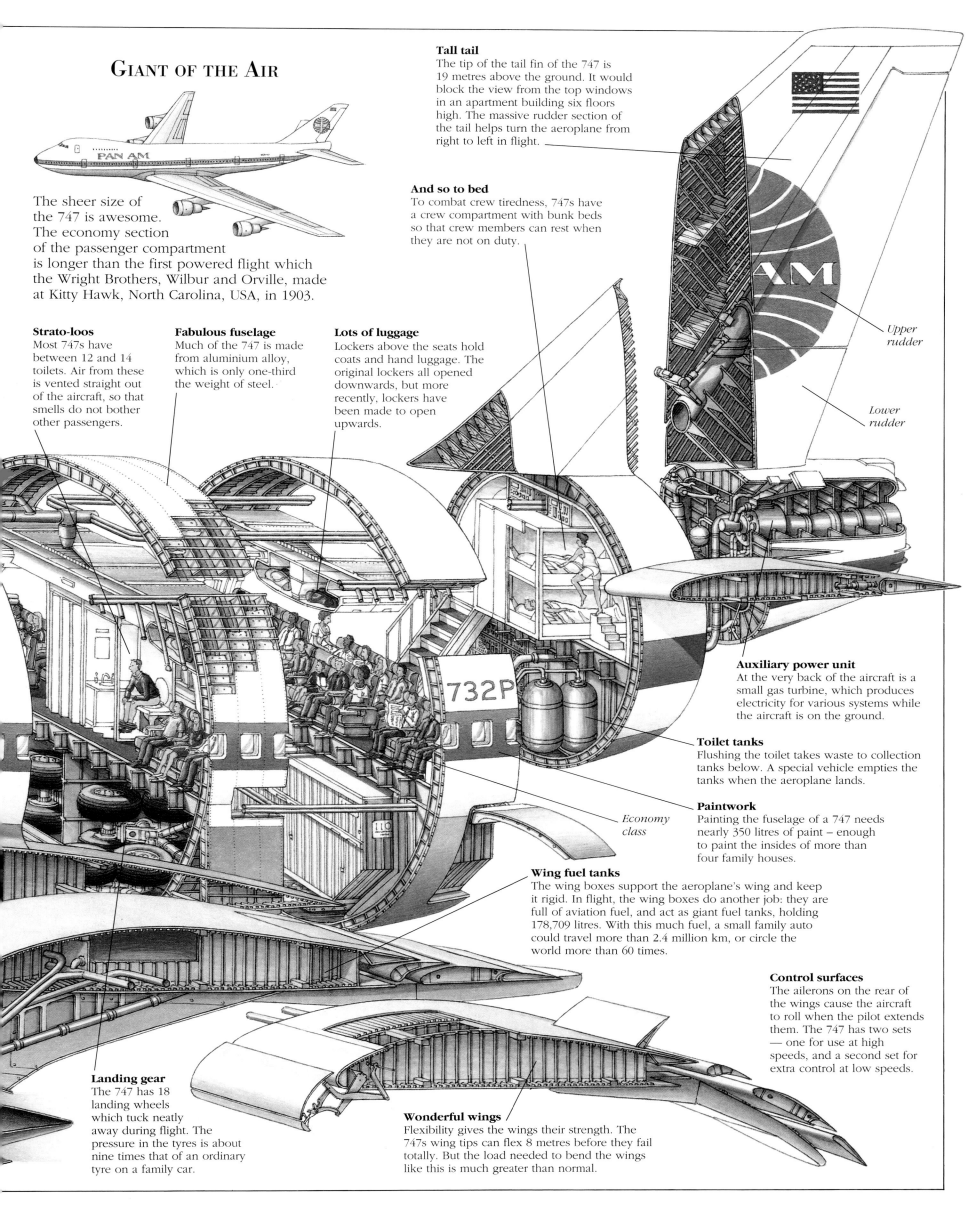

GIANT OF THE AIR

The sheer size of the 747 is awesome. The economy section of the passenger compartment is longer than the first powered flight which the Wright Brothers, Wilbur and Orville, made at Kitty Hawk, North Carolina, USA, in 1903.

Tall tail
The tip of the tail fin of the 747 is 19 metres above the ground. It would block the view from the top windows in an apartment building six floors high. The massive rudder section of the tail helps turn the aeroplane from right to left in flight.

And so to bed
To combat crew tiredness, 747s have a crew compartment with bunk beds so that crew members can rest when they are not on duty.

Strato-loos
Most 747s have between 12 and 14 toilets. Air from these is vented straight out of the aircraft, so that smells do not bother other passengers.

Fabulous fuselage
Much of the 747 is made from aluminium alloy, which is only one-third the weight of steel.

Lots of luggage
Lockers above the seats hold coats and hand luggage. The original lockers all opened downwards, but more recently, lockers have been made to open upwards.

Upper rudder

Lower rudder

Auxiliary power unit
At the very back of the aircraft is a small gas turbine, which produces electricity for various systems while the aircraft is on the ground.

Toilet tanks
Flushing the toilet takes waste to collection tanks below. A special vehicle empties the tanks when the aeroplane lands.

Economy class

Paintwork
Painting the fuselage of a 747 needs nearly 350 litres of paint – enough to paint the insides of more than four family houses.

Wing fuel tanks
The wing boxes support the aeroplane's wing and keep it rigid. In flight, the wing boxes do another job: they are full of aviation fuel, and act as giant fuel tanks, holding 178,709 litres. With this much fuel, a small family auto could travel more than 2.4 million km, or circle the world more than 60 times.

Control surfaces
The ailerons on the rear of the wings cause the aircraft to roll when the pilot extends them. The 747 has two sets — one for use at high speeds, and a second set for extra control at low speeds.

Landing gear
The 747 has 18 landing wheels which tuck neatly away during flight. The pressure in the tyres is about nine times that of an ordinary tyre on a family car.

Wonderful wings
Flexibility gives the wings their strength. The 747s wing tips can flex 8 metres before they fail totally. But the load needed to bend the wings like this is much greater than normal.

CAR FACTORY

Some people would say that robots make ideal factory workers. They don't stop for food, they don't get sick, they don't need to sleep, and they don't get bored. They are especially suited to factories that produce many similar products, such as cars. In a car factory, robots can do almost all the repetitive and physically tiring work. They lift, assemble, weld, spray paint, and perform many other tasks.

However, robots are not good at solving problems. When things go wrong, robots cannot cope. So today's factories still need human beings to keep production flowing smoothly and to control quality.

Press shop
The section of the factory where body and floor panels are made is called the press shop.

Roll up!
Metal for the car's panels arrives in rolls. It is coated with anti-corrosion chemicals. A remote-control crane unloads the roll from the lorries.

A pressing appointment
To shape the panels, the steel passes through a series of presses, each the height of a two storey house.

Dies
The presses squash the steel sheet between dies — pairs of curved steel moulds. Dies in the first press curve the metal gently. Each die that follows increases the curve. The last press squeezes the steel to the shape of the body panel, and trims excess metal.

Body shop
Panels move into storage before assembly into a "body-in-white". This is a complete unpainted body, without the engine, wheels, trim, and other components.

Checking with lasers
To check that the assembly process is working perfectly, sample bodies are measured using a laser scanner. This measures the body at 350 points to ensure that it is exactly the right size.

Paint shop
It takes 25 hours to paint each body. Many different steps are needed to create a perfect finish. There isn't room to show them all, but preparation before painting requires 11 separate steps to clean the steel and provide a base for the paint.

Primer bath

Drying oven

Paint tanks

Cutter
A powerful cutter slices rectangles of steel from the large roll.

Recycling trimmings
Excess steel cut from the panel drops onto a conveyor belt to be collected and recycled.

Safety guard
Gates keep people away from machines while they are operating. If workers try to operate machines with the gates open, an alarm sounds.

Positioning panels
Robot arms lift the body panels, and position them on a jig — a framework that holds all the panels.

Quality control
Human workers monitor quality in the factory. For instance, computers check the electrical current being fed to the welders, and alert human workers when it varies so they can adjust it.

Robot welder
Robots first spot-weld the panels (stick them together by melting the metal with a very hot electric spark). Then other robots add more spot-welds to finish the joint.

Attaching a transponder
The factory must control the number of car types made. Each body has a transponder (radio transmitter/receiver) which will identify it throughout the production stages that follow.

First dip
After careful preparation, the body plunges into a bath which coats it with primer paint. This protects the body from corrosion, and ensures that the paint will stick to it.

Bake in the oven until done
Between coats of paint, the body roasts in an oven at 82°C. After the final coat, the paint dries in an oven at 160°C.

A glossy finish
The car's transponder tells robots what colour it has got to be, and the robots spray on the right paint.

Don't slam the door!
After painting, the doors are removed for the next stage. This makes access to the car interior easier, and simplifies assembly of the doors.

Robo-carrier
Doors move through the production process on robo-carriers. These are miniature transport robots that move the doors along while workers add components to them. Robo-carriers also transport components around the plant, following cables buried in the floor.

Finished doors
The doors rejoin their car body as it emerges from the components/trim shop.

Components/trim shop
In this section of the factory the car begins to look more like a car, and less like a coloured shell. Here most of the electrics are added, and the passenger compartment is furnished and finished.

Fitting electrics
Small components such as lights reach the area where they are fitted on a "just-in-time" basis. Stocks of components on the production line are kept low to save space. The transponder attached to each body automatically orders the right parts as the body approaches. A robot finds the component, and delivers it just in time to be fitted.

The marriage conveyor
As the car nears the end of the production process, the body is married (joined) to the engine, steering, suspension, and transmission (the gearbox and related parts).

Rolling road
Running the car on rollers allows testers to check the engine and to make sure the brakes are working.

Wax coating
One last coat of wax protects the underbody from stone chips and damage by road salt.

Valeting
Polishing gives the car its show room shine.

Overhead conveyor
Like many parts in the factory, seats move from the trim shop to the production line on overhead conveyors.

Trim shop
This is the only area of the factory that has not been changed by robots. Here, workers cut and stitch carpets and seats using heavy-duty sewing machines.

Building engines
Some parts are manufactured in this factory, but others — even whole gearboxes — may be built in factories thousands of km away.

Fitting wheels
Workers fit the wheels by hand, but they are helped by a tool that tightens all the wheel nuts at once.

Testing, testing
Many of the car's components have been tested as they were manufactured and fitted — for example, by filling the fuel tank with air and immersing it in water checks for leaks. However, each car gets a thorough check before it goes out to be sold.

Don't forget the transponder
The transponder comes off now, and goes back to the beginning of the production line.

Road test
Finally the finished car goes off for a road test.

HELICOPTER

A loudspeaker at the Air-Sea Rescue base in southern England blares, "Scramble, scramble!" and the duty aircrew rub their eyes and stretch to wake up. The "scramble" message tells them that sleep is finished for the night, and they must go to work. For these four men, work means saving lives. Outside the window there is a gale blowing, a ship is sinking, and help is needed urgently or lives may be lost.

Before taking off, the crew need to carefully prepare their *Sea King* helicopter. But then the *Sea King* speeds them to their target at up to 250 km/h. At the ship it hovers while one of the crew is lowered on a cable to pluck the sailors from the deck. Then the *Sea King* rushes the crew and survivors back to the Air-Sea Rescue base.

Engine fire extinguisher bottles
The pilot can fill the engine compartment with foam to extinguish a fire there.

Blade pitch control rods
Rods connect the rotor blades to the swash plate. When the swash plate moves, the angle or pitch of the rotor blades changes.

Swash plate
The pilot's controls raise and lower the swash plate and alter its angle. Raising the swash plate increases the pitch of the rotors to provide more lift. Tilting the swash plate increases the helicopter's speed, or changes its direction.

Rotor

Engine air intakes

Oil cooler fan

Pass the apricots, please
Objects entering the engine can cause damage, so a guard protects the air intake. Salt spray can also cause problems. One solution is to spray some engine parts with a mixture of chemicals and ground apricot stones!

Turbine
Power for the *Sea King* comes from two Rolls-Royce Gnome turbine engines. If one engine fails, the helicopter can return to base using the other.

Pilot
The captain of the *Sea King* is usually the pilot, although sometimes the radar operator or navigator is in charge of the helicopter.

Cyclic pitch lever
Moving the cyclic pitch lever tilts the helicopter's rotor. The *Sea King* moves in the direction in which the rotor is tilted. For example, pushing the lever forward moves the helicopter forward.

Collective pitch lever
The controls on this lever alter both the engine speed and the pitch of the rotors. Operating them together makes the helicopter go up or down.

Co-pilot
The responsibilities of the co-pilot include navigation, pre-flight planning, and briefing the captain.

Yaw control
Pedals on the cabin floor control yaw — rotation of the helicopter to the left or right.

Radio and electronics equipment
Much of the helicopter's electronic equipment is mounted below the pilot and co-pilot's feet.

Radar operator
Navigation equipment and radar are the responsibility of the radar operator, who sits behind the pilot.

Fuel
With a full tank of fuel, the latest *Sea King* helicopters have a range of more than 1,400 km.

Oxygen bottles
Every search and rescue helicopter carries a good first-aid kit, including oxygen cylinders. All members of the crew are trained in first aid.

Water wings
If the helicopter comes down over water, emergency flotation bags inflate with compressed air to prevent the helicopter from sinking.

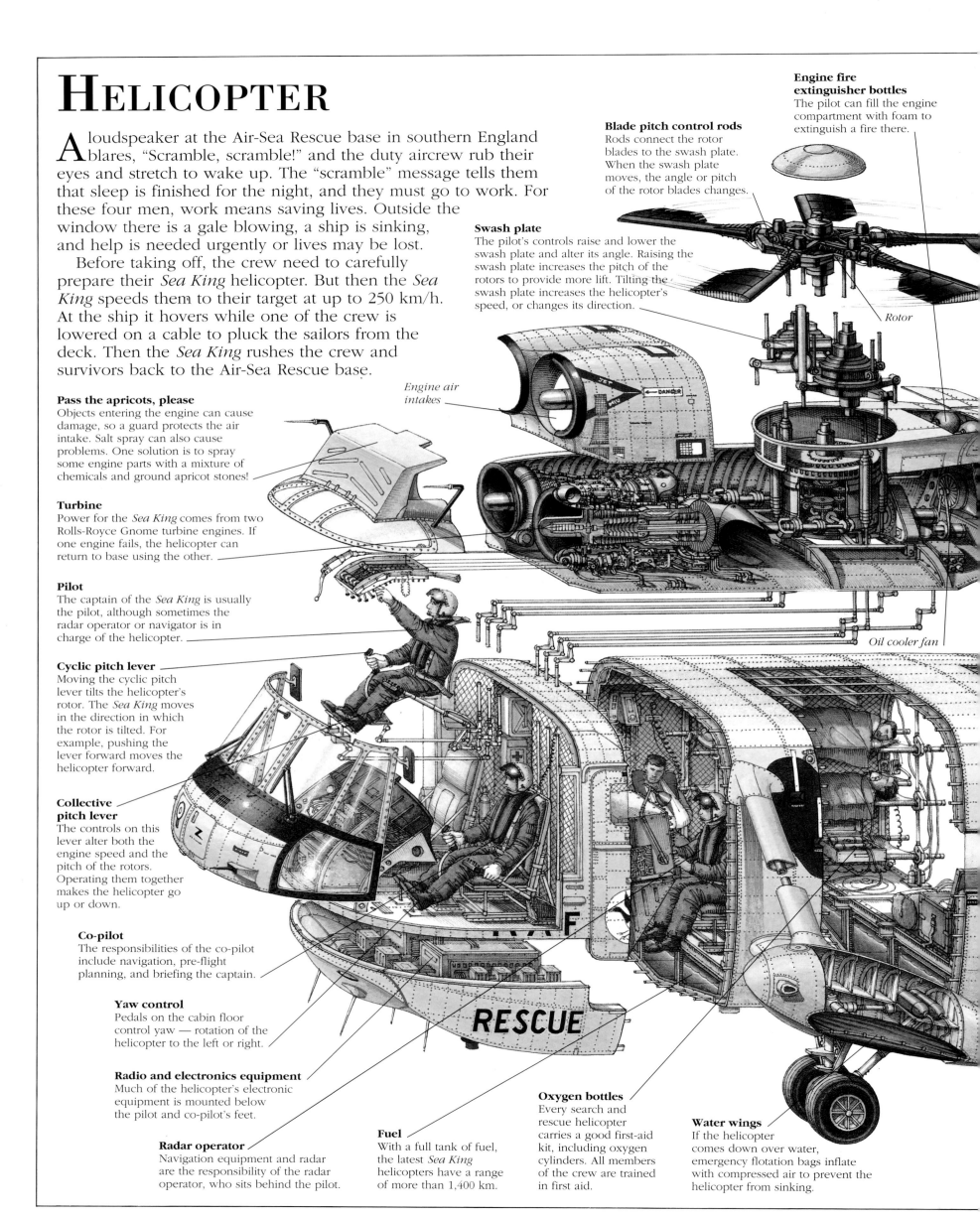

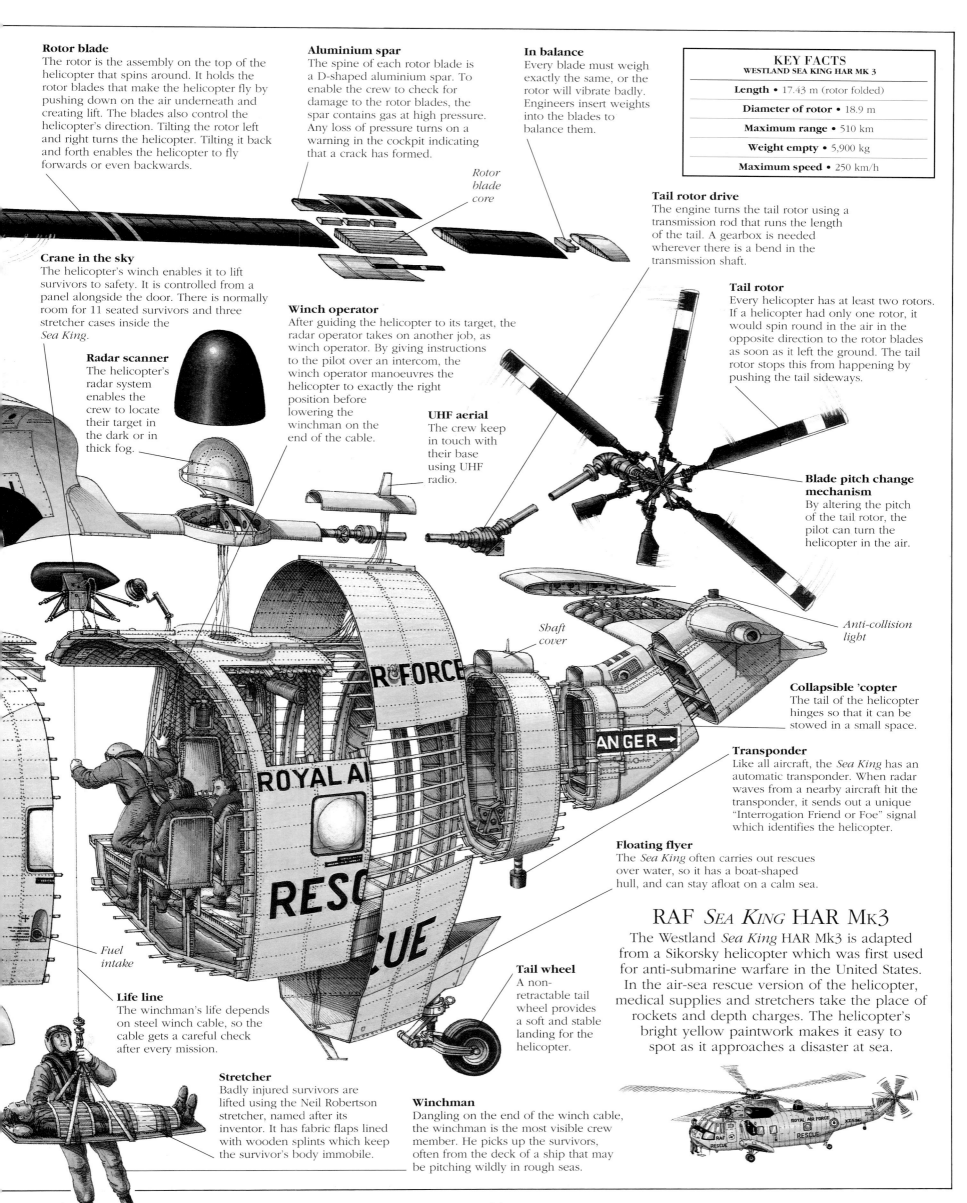

Rotor blade
The rotor is the assembly on the top of the helicopter that spins around. It holds the rotor blades that make the helicopter fly by pushing down on the air underneath and creating lift. The blades also control the helicopter's direction. Tilting the rotor left and right turns the helicopter. Tilting it back and forth enables the helicopter to fly forwards or even backwards.

Aluminium spar
The spine of each rotor blade is a D-shaped aluminium spar. To enable the crew to check for damage to the rotor blades, the spar contains gas at high pressure. Any loss of pressure turns on a warning in the cockpit indicating that a crack has formed.

Rotor blade core

In balance
Every blade must weigh exactly the same, or the rotor will vibrate badly. Engineers insert weights into the blades to balance them.

KEY FACTS
WESTLAND SEA KING HAR MK 3

Length	• 17.43 m (rotor folded)
Diameter of rotor	• 18.9 m
Maximum range	• 510 km
Weight empty	• 5,900 kg
Maximum speed	• 250 km/h

Tail rotor drive
The engine turns the tail rotor using a transmission rod that runs the length of the tail. A gearbox is needed wherever there is a bend in the transmission shaft.

Crane in the sky
The helicopter's winch enables it to lift survivors to safety. It is controlled from a panel alongside the door. There is normally room for 11 seated survivors and three stretcher cases inside the *Sea King*.

Radar scanner
The helicopter's radar system enables the crew to locate their target in the dark or in thick fog.

Winch operator
After guiding the helicopter to its target, the radar operator takes on another job, as winch operator. By giving instructions to the pilot over an intercom, the winch operator manoeuvres the helicopter to exactly the right position before lowering the winchman on the end of the cable.

UHF aerial
The crew keep in touch with their base using UHF radio.

Tail rotor
Every helicopter has at least two rotors. If a helicopter had only one rotor, it would spin round in the air in the opposite direction to the rotor blades as soon as it left the ground. The tail rotor stops this from happening by pushing the tail sideways.

Blade pitch change mechanism
By altering the pitch of the tail rotor, the pilot can turn the helicopter in the air.

Shaft cover

Anti-collision light

Collapsible 'copter
The tail of the helicopter hinges so that it can be stowed in a small space.

Transponder
Like all aircraft, the *Sea King* has an automatic transponder. When radar waves from a nearby aircraft hit the transponder, it sends out a unique "Interrogation Friend or Foe" signal which identifies the helicopter.

Floating flyer
The *Sea King* often carries out rescues over water, so it has a boat-shaped hull, and can stay afloat on a calm sea.

Fuel intake

Life line
The winchman's life depends on steel winch cable, so the cable gets a careful check after every mission.

Tail wheel
A non-retractable tail wheel provides a soft and stable landing for the helicopter.

RAF *SEA KING* HAR MK3
The Westland *Sea King* HAR Mk3 is adapted from a Sikorsky helicopter which was first used for anti-submarine warfare in the United States. In the air-sea rescue version of the helicopter, medical supplies and stretchers take the place of rockets and depth charges. The helicopter's bright yellow paintwork makes it easy to spot as it approaches a disaster at sea.

Stretcher
Badly injured survivors are lifted using the Neil Robertson stretcher, named after its inventor. It has fabric flaps lined with wooden splints which keep the survivor's body immobile.

Winchman
Dangling on the end of the winch cable, the winchman is the most visible crew member. He picks up the survivors, often from the deck of a ship that may be pitching wildly in rough seas.

OPERA HOUSE

When you step inside an opera house, you leave reality behind with your coat. Like a magic spell, the action on the stage transports you to another land, another time, or another world. From the auditorium (the area where you sit and watch), operatic productions seem effortless, graceful, and glamorous. But the glitter of the stage is a beautiful and pleasant illusion.

Keeping up the illusion is hard work, as an operatic production involves singers and instrumentalists and can also include dancers and extras. There is also an army of other workers who make and paint sets, sew costumes, and sell tickets. All day long around the building the magic spell of opera is created with paint, cloth, wood, sheets of music, and hours of tiring rehearsal.

Meet me in the saloon
Above the foyer is a large, richly-decorated room called the grand saloon. Here members of the audience can meet, see and be seen before the performance.

Crush bar
During the interval everybody hurries to the bar to buy drinks. It gets very crowded, so it's called the crush bar.

Columns
The grand white columns at the front of the opera house are more than 18 m high.

Main entrance

Rehearsal room
Every bit of space in the opera house is used as efficiently as possible. Here a rehearsal room is tucked in behind the pediment – the triangular portion under the roof.

Lighting booth
The lighting crew sit high up in a booth that gives them a view of the whole stage. From here they help control the lighting effects.

Opera for everyone
The cheapest seats in the auditorium are in the slips – narrow spaces at the top and sides of the theatre. The view is not very good, but prices are kept low so that anyone can afford them.

Carpentry shop
Space in the roof is used for workshops, including the carpentry shop where workers create stage props.

Spotlights
Powerful spotlights pick out individual performers on the stage. By turning the lamps, the lighting technicians can follow the performers with a small pool of light as they move around.

Foyer
The foyer is where the audience members enter from the street, buy their programmes, and leave their coats.

Café

Storage area

Stalls
The most expensive place to sit in the opera house is in the stalls. But here you get the best view, and you can hear the music better than anywhere else in the auditorium.

Orchestra
The musicians sit between the stage and the audience, in the orchestra pit. They face towards the conductor, who uses gestures to lead both the musicians in the pit, and the performers on the stage.

What's my line?
In the centre of the stage is the prompt booth where the prompter follows the words of the opera from a score (the words and music of the opera). If anyone forgets their words, the prompter reminds them.

Royal box
The best seats in the opera house are reserved for the royal family. They are in a private box at the side of the stage.

Royal rooms
Royal visitors have a suite of rooms below their box, where they can sit in comfort before the performance, and during the interval.

A supporting role
Eight huge girders support the roof. Each weighs 30 tonnes. The girders were prefabricated (constructed separately from the rest of the building) in a factory 170 km from the opera house.

Lighting
Powerful lamps hang from gantries (long hanging racks) above the stage.

Costume storage
Designing and making costumes is a huge task: everybody in the cast has at least one costume.

Painting room
Because backdrops are so big, there is a huge room for painting them. This one is for Verdi's opera *Aida,* set in Egypt.

Chorus rehearsal room
A choir, called the chorus, sing some of the opera on their own, and also sometimes accompany the opera soloists. The chorus practise in a large room at the back of the building.

Score store
Every member of the cast needs a copy of the words and music of the opera and there is a different part for each musical instrument in the orchestra. So the opera house has a library containing all the different parts for many operas.

Ballet practice room
The ballet dancers must practise for many hours a day to keep their bodies supple. They have a rehearsal room high up behind the stage.

ROYAL OPERA HOUSE, COVENT GARDEN

The Royal Opera House in London, England is among the finest in the world. It is more than 130 years old, and replaced an older building on the same site that was burned down in a fire. The building was completed very quickly, taking only seven months from start to finish.

Ballet dancers practising

Fan club
Opera fans wait at the stage door after a show hoping for a glimpse of their heroes leaving.

Foundations

A big noise
Down below the stage is a big room where the orchestra rehearse, and where they store large instruments such as harps and pianos.

Strike a light
To control the stage lights, there is a lighting board at the sides of the stage. From here, the electricians can switch the lights on and off at the correct moment.

Switch room
The opera house uses a lot of electricity, and the switch room controls its distribution.

Trap
The stage has five traps, or small lifts. To make a sudden appearance, a performer stands on a lowered trap beneath the stage. On cue (at the right instant in the production) stage hands operate the trap, and the performer is hoisted rapidly upwards to stage level.

Lift
The opera house is nine storeys high, so a lift is essential.

Gentlemen's chorus dressing room

Ladies' chorus dressing room
The members of the chorus all share a big dressing room. The costume staff have to start early in the day, washing, repairing, and pressing the many costumes.

Solo artists' dressing rooms
Only solo singers, or principals, have a dressing room all to themselves. The rooms are tiny, but well-known opera stars have a suite of rooms — a dressing room, and a sitting room where they can entertain friends and fans.

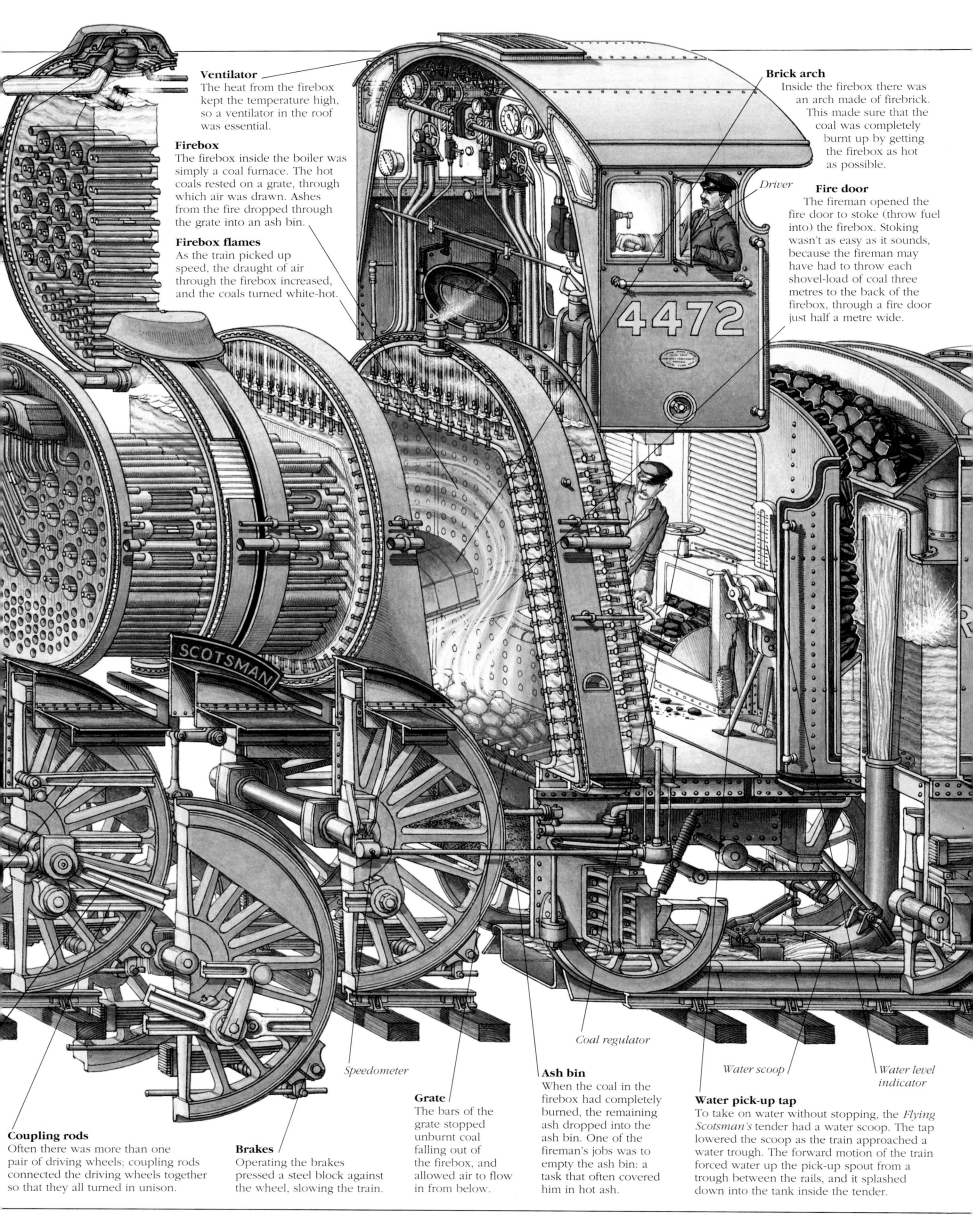

Ventilator
The heat from the firebox kept the temperature high, so a ventilator in the roof was essential.

Firebox
The firebox inside the boiler was simply a coal furnace. The hot coals rested on a grate, through which air was drawn. Ashes from the fire dropped through the grate into an ash bin.

Firebox flames
As the train picked up speed, the draught of air through the firebox increased, and the coals turned white-hot.

Brick arch
Inside the firebox there was an arch made of firebrick. This made sure that the coal was completely burnt up by getting the firebox as hot as possible.

Driver

Fire door
The fireman opened the fire door to stoke (throw fuel into) the firebox. Stoking wasn't as easy as it sounds, because the fireman may have had to throw each shovel-load of coal three metres to the back of the firebox, through a fire door just half a metre wide.

SCOTSMAN

4472

Coal regulator

Speedometer

Grate
The bars of the grate stopped unburnt coal falling out of the firebox, and allowed air to flow in from below.

Ash bin
When the coal in the firebox had completely burned, the remaining ash dropped into the ash bin. One of the fireman's jobs was to empty the ash bin: a task that often covered him in hot ash.

Water scoop

Water level indicator

Water pick-up tap
To take on water without stopping, the *Flying Scotsman's* tender had a water scoop. The tap lowered the scoop as the train approached a water trough. The forward motion of the train forced water up the pick-up spout from a trough between the rails, and it splashed down into the tank inside the tender.

Coupling rods
Often there was more than one pair of driving wheels; coupling rods connected the driving wheels together so that they all turned in unison.

Brakes
Operating the brakes pressed a steel block against the wheel, slowing the train.

STEAM TRAIN

Breathing fire, steam, and smoke, a steam train was like a dragon on rails. To bring this dragon to life, though, demanded loving care and attention, and hard work. The crew at the engine shed had to start work many hours before the train was due to depart. They lit a fire in the firebox, and when it was ablaze, they fed it with coal until the whole firebox was a roaring inferno. Gradually the heat warmed the water in the boiler which surrounded the firebox. As the water got hotter, it turned to steam. Locomotives had a crew of two: a driver and a fireman. They took over from the engine shed crew when it was time to drive the train.

When the steam pressure was high enough, the driver opened the regulator valve, allowing steam into the locomotive's cylinders. The steam pressure forced the pistons back and forth, and they moved the driving rods linked to the wheels. Slowly, the huge locomotive inched forward in the dawn, and gradually picked up speed — then passengers or freight. Finally, with a shrill blast on the whistle, the locomotive steamed off into the distance, hauling up to 700 tonnes of carriages or goods wagons at speeds up to 160 km/h.

The 1930s were golden years of steam railway travel. In Great Britain, gorgeously-painted locomotives such as the London and North Eastern Railway's 4472 *Flying Scotsman* shown here pulled luxurious carriages non-stop over great distances. The passengers in those carriages enjoyed first-class meals, sleeping car accommodation, showers, and novelties such as headsets and even a cinema car. Eventually, though, cheap road and air travel made the costs of running such lavish trains too great. This, and the expense of fighting World War II (1939-45) meant that such passenger luxury was only rarely, if ever, seen again.

FLYING SCOTSMAN

The *Flying Scotsman* locomotive shown here was designed by Sir Nigel Gresley (1876-1941). Gresley designed several famous locomotives for the London and North Eastern Railway. Number 4472 was part of a class of locomotive that dated from 1923. One of Gresley's later locomotives, 4468 *Mallard*, still holds the speed record for a steam locomotive — 202 km/h — reached in a test run in 1938. Both *Flying Scotsman* and *Mallard* are preserved today.

Driver's controls
By comparison with the cab of a modern diesel locomotive, the footplate of the *Flying Scotsman* has remarkably few instruments. A speedometer, simple pressure and temperature gauges, and water level indicators gave the driver and fireman all the information they needed. At night, tiny oil lamps illuminated the controls.

Boiler tubes
Hot flue gases from the firebox flowed along many pipes that passed through the water jacket, so that the maximum possible area of water came into contact with the heat.

Chimney
Smoke from the firebox and waste steam from the cylinders rose from the locomotive's chimney in great clouds with each piston stroke, giving the locomotive its familiar "chuff-chuff" noise.

Superheater tubes
Steam from the boiler passed into superheater tubes. These made the steam even hotter, increasing its pressure, so that it could push harder on the pistons, improving the efficiency of the locomotive.

Smokebox door

Lamp
A warning lamp on the front of the locomotive ensured that it was visible at night.

Blast pipe
Steam from the cylinders flowed out of the blast pipe and up the chimney. Because the smokebox door was closed so tightly, a partial vacuum was created which drew the waste gases from the firebox through the fire tubes and up the chimney. This process made air enter the firebox, and the fire burn hotter.

Steam dome and regulator valve
Steam in the boiler collected in the steam space above the water. Steam in the dome was at the highest point away from the water level and was thus the driest steam. The regulator valve was housed in the dome. The driver used this valve like the throttle on a car: opening the valve propelled the locomotive forward (or backward).

Boiler wall
The boiler was made from strong steel sheets, so that it could withstand the high pressure of the steam inside.

Regulator valve

Cylinder valve
Steam can only *push* the cylinder, it cannot pull it. So to make the cylinder oscillate (move alternately backward and forward), an arrangement of valves let the steam flow into the cylinder first at one side of the piston, and then at the other.

Cylinders
Superheated steam passed into cylinders, where it pressed on pistons which drove the wheels via connecting rods. On the *Flying Scotsman* there were three cylinders: one on each side, and a third cylinder between the wheels.

Valve rods
Another set of rods coordinated the opening and closing of the steam valves which controlled the flow of steam into the cylinders.

Driving rods
Heavy steel rods transferred the movement of the pistons to the wheels that drove the locomotive forward.

STEAM TRAIN

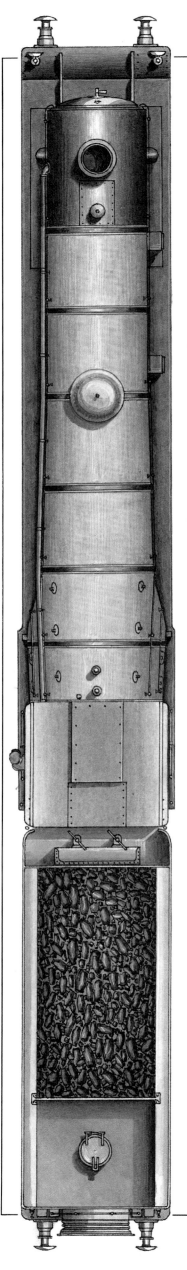

When steam trains first appeared, around 1830, they were as exciting as space travel is today. They terrified some people, who feared for their health. One writer commented: *"What can be more ridiculous than locomotives travelling twice as fast as stage coaches? We should as soon expect people to suffer themselves to be fired off on rockets as trust themselves to the mercy of a machine going at such a rate."* Pleading for sanity, he demanded that railway trains should be limited to a speed of eight or nine miles an hour. Others declared that locomotives would *"kill the birds, prevent cows from grazing and hens from laying, burn houses, and cause the extinction of the race of horses"*. All these critics were proved wrong, and by the middle of the 20th century, the steam train reigned as the most sophisticated way of travelling by land. Pullman passengers (those travelling in the most luxurious class) could enjoy an invigorating shower, a first-class meal, or watch the latest film in the train's cinema.

LOCOMOTIVE

The locomotive shown here belonged to England's London and North Eastern Railway. It was numbered 4472 and named *Flying Scotsman*. It is a "Pacific" class locomotive — a typical passenger express locomotive of the 1920s and 1930s. "Pacific" class locomotives had a set of six large linked driving wheels in the centre, with four free running wheels in front and two free running wheels at the rear.

Side view showing wheel arrangement

BIRD'S-EYE VIEW

A torrent of steam and smoke would normally have hidden the locomotive from view as it passed under bridges. The nine tonnes of coal in the tender was used as fuel for non-stop journeys.

Top view of locomotive and tender

Side view of restaurant carriage

FLYING SCOTSMAN TRAIN

Both a locomotive and a train were called *Flying Scotsman*. The *Flying Scotsman* express train travelled from London, England to Edinburgh, Scotland — a distance of 630 km. It travelled non-stop from May 1928, making it then the longest non-stop service in the world.

EDINBURGH   DISTANCE IN KILOMETRES

| 0 | 60 | 120 | 180 | 240 | 300 |

Front view showing smokebox door

FOOTPLATE

The controls of the locomotive are on the footplate. The driver's view ahead was often obscured by steam or smoke. The fireman fed the fire with coal. He also had to learn the train's route, so he would know when to stoke up the fire to provide more power.

TENDER

Steam locomotives ran on coal and water. The locomotive's tender carried a supply of both. It also had a corridor which allowed a relief crew to walk through and replace the driver and fireman without stopping.

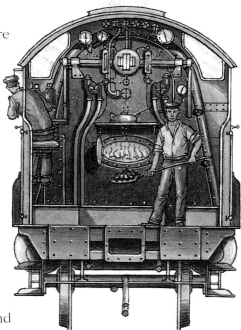

Footplate view showing controls

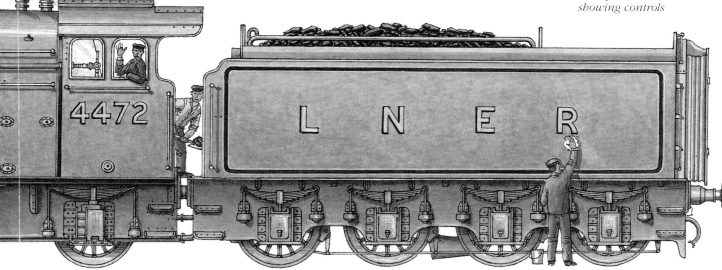

LOOKING UP

This is the view that the maintenance crew had in the engine shed when they crawled underneath the locomotive to remove ash from the firebox grate.

Bottom view of locomotive and tender

CARRIAGES

Carriages were built by skilled workers, mainly using a framework of teak wood. By the 1930s, when the carriage shown above was built, many parts were made of steel. Some later steel-shelled carriages were then actually painted to look like teak!

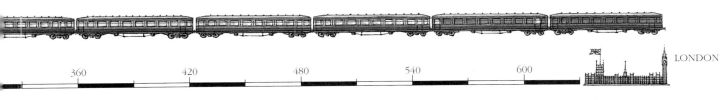

360   420   480   540   600   LONDON

Ten-car set
Carriages were coupled in sets of 8, 10, 12, or even 14. *The carriages shown here are a selection to show the types of travel available to passengers in the 1930s. They do not represent an actual train make-up.*

Cocktail bar
Cocktails were among the most fashionable drinks in the 1930s. So there was a cocktail bar, complete with bar stools. These were fixed to the floor in case the combination of strong drinks and the train's motion should cause unsteadiness in those at the bar.

Travelling Post Office (TPO)
The railway was a vital link in the mail distribution network. On some trains postmen sorted letters during the journey, to reduce delivery time.

Carriage construction
In the 1930s steel carriages began to supersede the older wooden types. Sometimes the steel was painted to look like wood.

Guard's van
Luggage that did not fit in the carriages travelled in the guard's van.

Line-side mail gantry
The Travelling Post Office could pick up mail bags without stopping. Post Office workers hung mail bags on a line-side gantry (support), and a special hook collected them as the train passed.

Hairdressing saloon
Both men and women could have their hair trimmed and styled on the train, and there was a waiting room so that passengers could queue in comfort.

Galley
The cramped galley (kitchen) had an electric cooker. However, the generators and batteries had limited capacity, so the roasting ovens were powered by a coal fire.

Lavatory
Flushing discharged the contents of the toilet bowl onto the track below, so maintenance staff walked alongside the rails, not between them.

WHO WAS ONBOARD
Express trains in the 1930s had a large complement of staff. The driver and fireman drove the locomotive. The guard looked after luggage and safe departures. The ticket inspector made sure everyone travelled in the right class of carriage. Stewards served the meals that the cooks prepared. The barber looked after the passengers' hairdressing requirements, and the projectionist showed films in the cinema car. Finally, post office staff sorted mail in the TPO.

THE CREW

Driver

Fireman

Guard

Ticket Inspector

Cooks

Stewards

Buffet Steward

Projectionist

Barber

Post Office Staff

THE PASSENGERS

72 1st Class

255 3rd Class

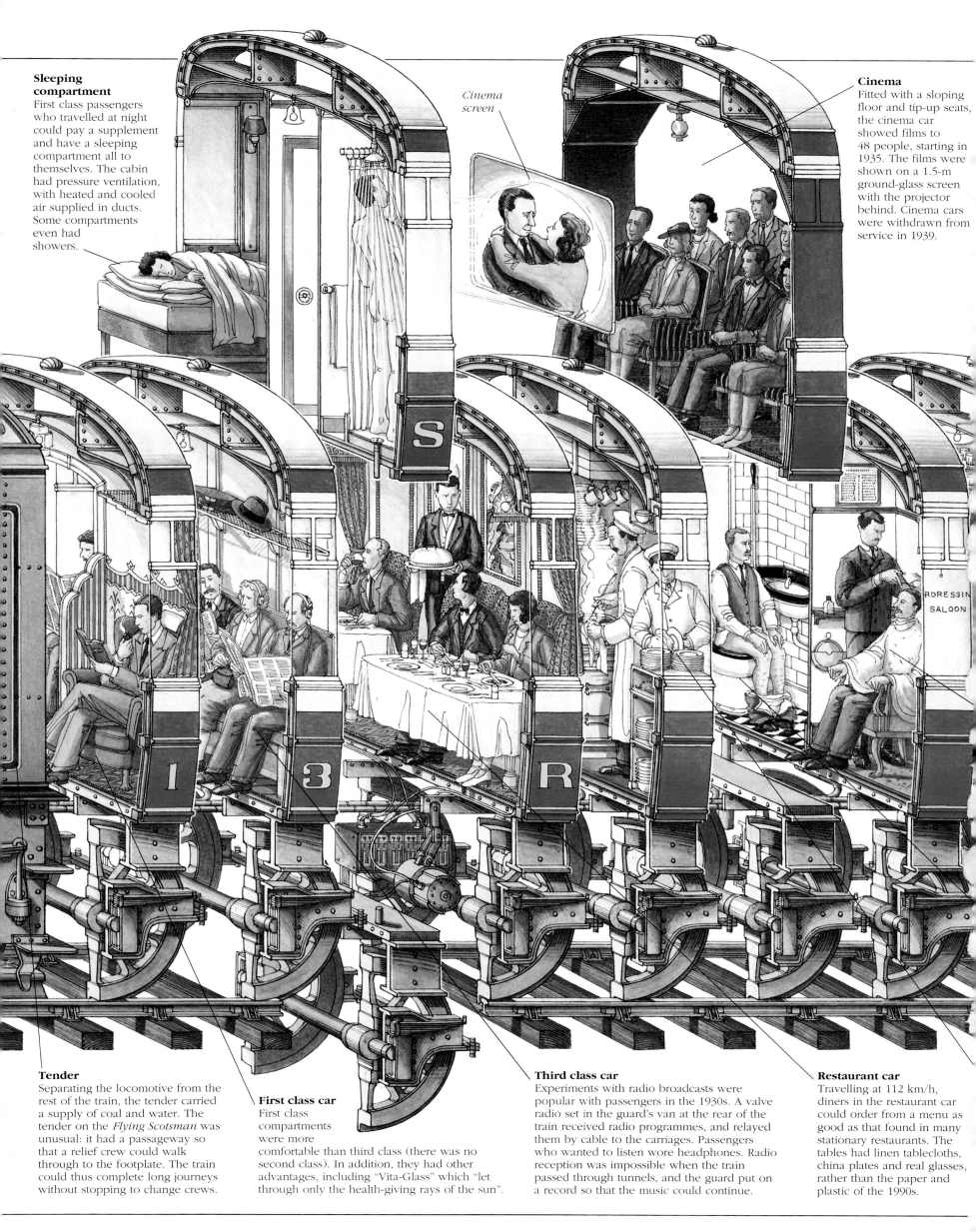

Sleeping compartment
First class passengers who travelled at night could pay a supplement and have a sleeping compartment all to themselves. The cabin had pressure ventilation, with heated and cooled air supplied in ducts. Some compartments even had showers.

Cinema screen

Cinema
Fitted with a sloping floor and tip-up seats, the cinema car showed films to 48 people, starting in 1935. The films were shown on a 1.5-m ground-glass screen with the projector behind. Cinema cars were withdrawn from service in 1939.

Tender
Separating the locomotive from the rest of the train, the tender carried a supply of coal and water. The tender on the *Flying Scotsman* was unusual: it had a passageway so that a relief crew could walk through to the footplate. The train could thus complete long journeys without stopping to change crews.

First class car
First class compartments were more comfortable than third class (there was no second class). In addition, they had other advantages, including "Vita-Glass" which "let through only the health-giving rays of the sun".

Third class car
Experiments with radio broadcasts were popular with passengers in the 1930s. A valve radio set in the guard's van at the rear of the train received radio programmes, and relayed them by cable to the carriages. Passengers who wanted to listen wore headphones. Radio reception was impossible when the train passed through tunnels, and the guard put on a record so that the music could continue.

Restaurant car
Travelling at 112 km/h, diners in the restaurant car could order from a menu as good as that found in many stationary restaurants. The tables had linen tablecloths, china plates and real glasses, rather than the paper and plastic of the 1990s.

SUBWAY STATION

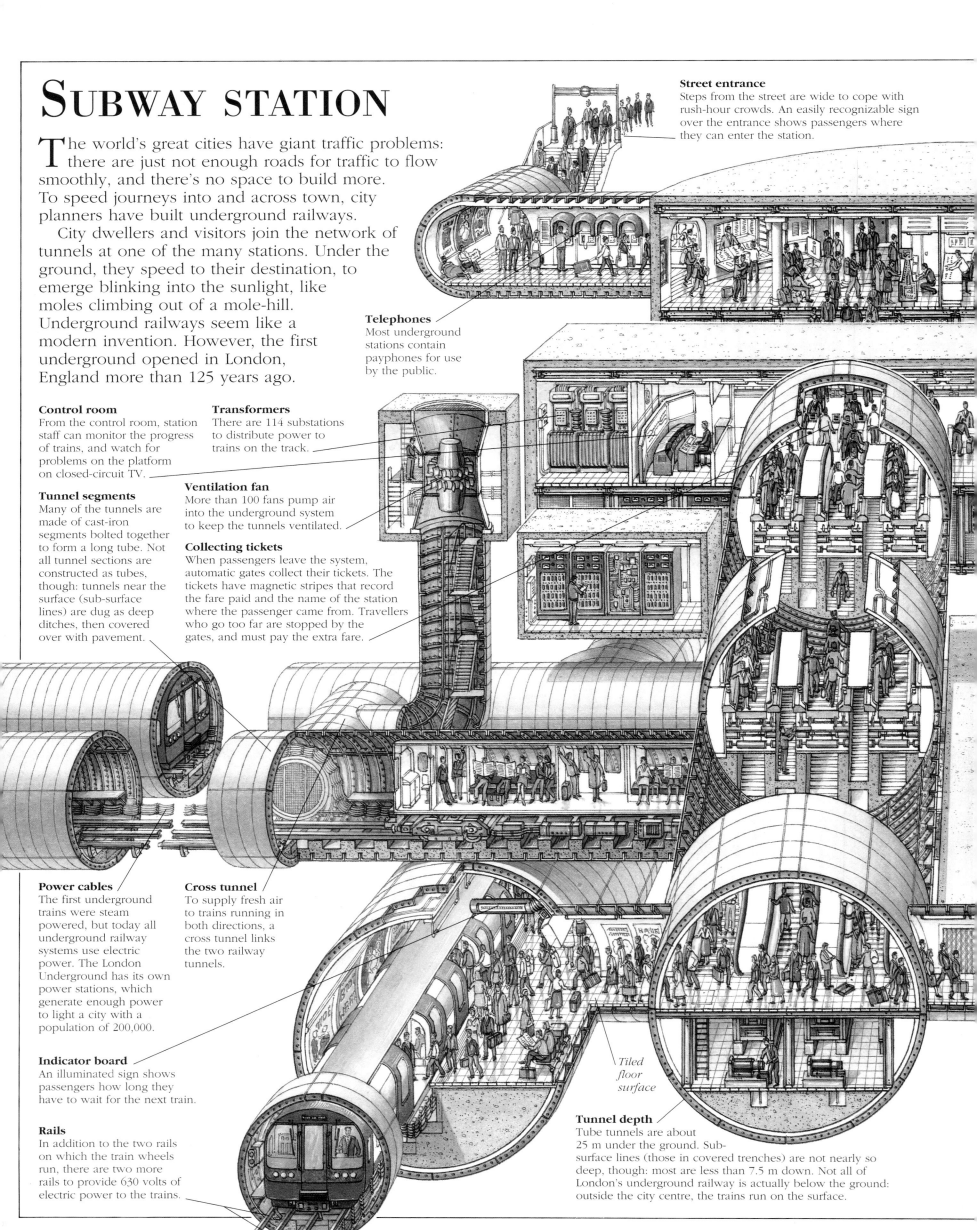

The world's great cities have giant traffic problems: there are just not enough roads for traffic to flow smoothly, and there's no space to build more. To speed journeys into and across town, city planners have built underground railways.

City dwellers and visitors join the network of tunnels at one of the many stations. Under the ground, they speed to their destination, to emerge blinking into the sunlight, like moles climbing out of a mole-hill. Underground railways seem like a modern invention. However, the first underground opened in London, England more than 125 years ago.

Street entrance
Steps from the street are wide to cope with rush-hour crowds. An easily recognizable sign over the entrance shows passengers where they can enter the station.

Telephones
Most underground stations contain payphones for use by the public.

Control room
From the control room, station staff can monitor the progress of trains, and watch for problems on the platform on closed-circuit TV.

Transformers
There are 114 substations to distribute power to trains on the track.

Tunnel segments
Many of the tunnels are made of cast-iron segments bolted together to form a long tube. Not all tunnel sections are constructed as tubes, though: tunnels near the surface (sub-surface lines) are dug as deep ditches, then covered over with pavement.

Ventilation fan
More than 100 fans pump air into the underground system to keep the tunnels ventilated.

Collecting tickets
When passengers leave the system, automatic gates collect their tickets. The tickets have magnetic stripes that record the fare paid and the name of the station where the passenger came from. Travellers who go too far are stopped by the gates, and must pay the extra fare.

Power cables
The first underground trains were steam powered, but today all underground railway systems use electric power. The London Underground has its own power stations, which generate enough power to light a city with a population of 200,000.

Cross tunnel
To supply fresh air to trains running in both directions, a cross tunnel links the two railway tunnels.

Indicator board
An illuminated sign shows passengers how long they have to wait for the next train.

Rails
In addition to the two rails on which the train wheels run, there are two more rails to provide 630 volts of electric power to the trains.

Tiled floor surface

Tunnel depth
Tube tunnels are about 25 m under the ground. Sub-surface lines (those in covered trenches) are not nearly so deep, though: most are less than 7.5 m down. Not all of London's underground railway is actually below the ground: outside the city centre, the trains run on the surface.

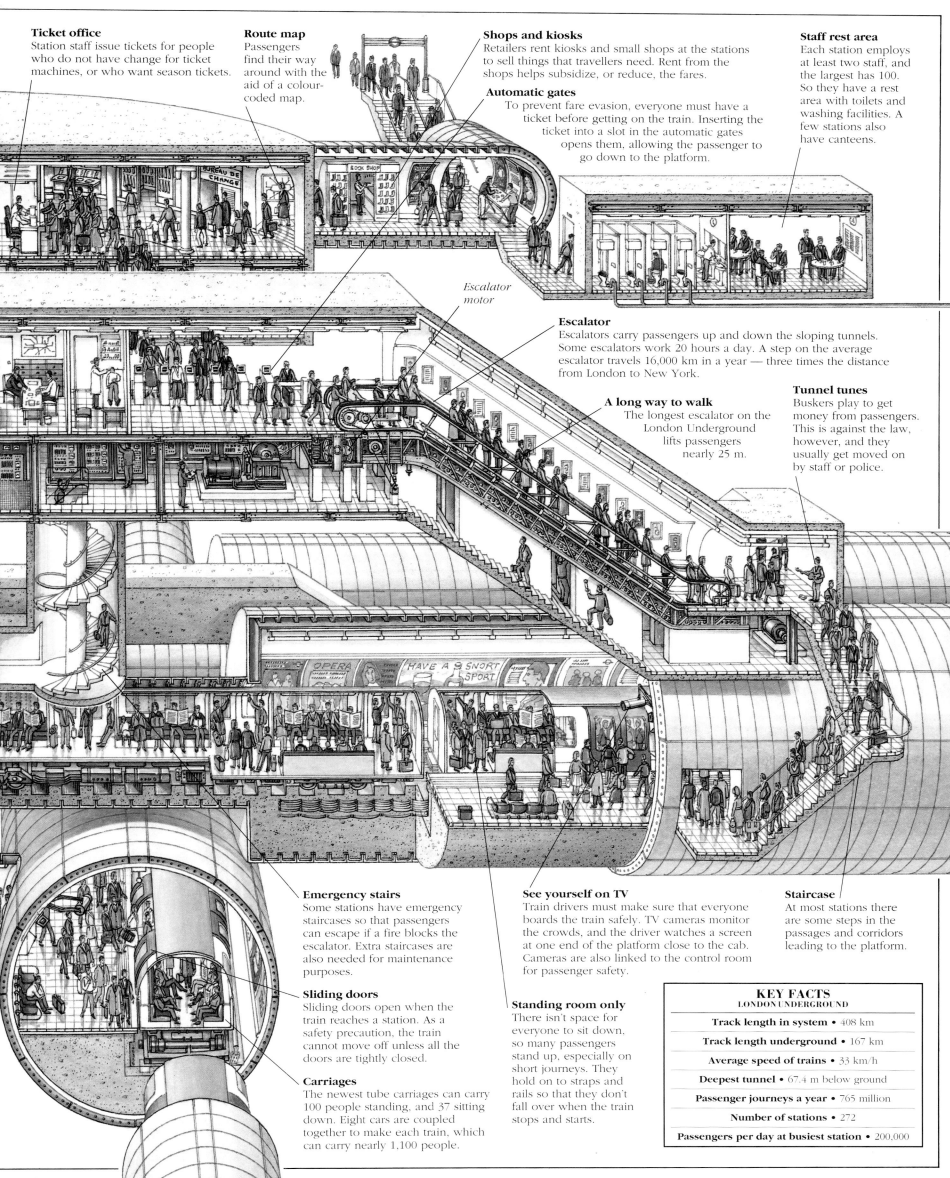

Ticket office
Station staff issue tickets for people who do not have change for ticket machines, or who want season tickets.

Route map
Passengers find their way around with the aid of a colour-coded map.

Shops and kiosks
Retailers rent kiosks and small shops at the stations to sell things that travellers need. Rent from the shops helps subsidize, or reduce, the fares.

Automatic gates
To prevent fare evasion, everyone must have a ticket before getting on the train. Inserting the ticket into a slot in the automatic gates opens them, allowing the passenger to go down to the platform.

Staff rest area
Each station employs at least two staff, and the largest has 100. So they have a rest area with toilets and washing facilities. A few stations also have canteens.

Escalator motor

Escalator
Escalators carry passengers up and down the sloping tunnels. Some escalators work 20 hours a day. A step on the average escalator travels 16,000 km in a year — three times the distance from London to New York.

A long way to walk
The longest escalator on the London Underground lifts passengers nearly 25 m.

Tunnel tunes
Buskers play to get money from passengers. This is against the law, however, and they usually get moved on by staff or police.

Emergency stairs
Some stations have emergency staircases so that passengers can escape if a fire blocks the escalator. Extra staircases are also needed for maintenance purposes.

Sliding doors
Sliding doors open when the train reaches a station. As a safety precaution, the train cannot move off unless all the doors are tightly closed.

Carriages
The newest tube carriages can carry 100 people standing, and 37 sitting down. Eight cars are coupled together to make each train, which can carry nearly 1,100 people.

See yourself on TV
Train drivers must make sure that everyone boards the train safely. TV cameras monitor the crowds, and the driver watches a screen at one end of the platform close to the cab. Cameras are also linked to the control room for passenger safety.

Standing room only
There isn't space for everyone to sit down, so many passengers stand up, especially on short journeys. They hold on to straps and rails so that they don't fall over when the train stops and starts.

Staircase
At most stations there are some steps in the passages and corridors leading to the platform.

KEY FACTS	
LONDON UNDERGROUND	
Track length in system • 408 km	
Track length underground • 167 km	
Average speed of trains • 33 km/h	
Deepest tunnel • 67.4 m below ground	
Passenger journeys a year • 765 million	
Number of stations • 272	
Passengers per day at busiest station • 200,000	

FISHING TRAWLER

Before farming began, people got their food by gathering grains and fruits, and by hunting wild animals. Today, much of our food comes from farms, but ocean fish are still hunted. Modern fishing ships are highly mechanized fish-hunting factories. But sadly, their success may bring ocean fishing to an end, because the fish that escape the nets cannot breed fast enough. Soon, even the most efficient fishing vessel will be useless, for there will be few fish left to catch.

Radar scanners
The rotating radar scanners enable the crew to detect other vessels many km away even when thick fog reduces visibility.

Bow gantry
The ship's two gantries support tackle that helps haul in the nets. The front of a ship is called the bow, so this is the bow gantry.

Pulleys
Pulleys strung between the gantries enable the crew to move the catch (the net full of fish) around the deck.

Hydraulic trawl winches
When the ship is towing the trawl, the crew use two large winches to pay out and haul in the trawl warps (the cables attached to the net).

Radio mast

Fishing lights
Fishing nets are a hazard to other vessels, so when fishing at night the trawler displays special warning lights.

Cable winch
A small winch below the bow gantry pulls the cables that move the nets around on deck.

Net drum
As it is emptied of fish, a net is wound onto the net drum for storage.

Reflector compass
The ship's compass on the top of the wheelhouse contains an optical system so that the bearing (the direction in which the ship is heading) can be seen clearly by the crew member steering the ship.

Radio room
The radio keeps the ship in contact with shore personnel. Many skippers prefer not to use the radio when they find good fishing grounds, because they fear that other ships will locate the spot from the radio signal.

Skipper
The master or captain of a trawler is called the skipper.

Wheelhouse
From the wheelhouse the helm has a good all-round view of the decks, and of the sea on all sides.

Life preserver
Stern trawlers are safer than the older side trawlers, but life preservers are still vital in case any of the crew fall overboard.

Searchlight

Accommodation
Space is very limited on the ship, and none of the crew has a large cabin, but the skipper and mate (his assistant) have a little more space.

Galley (Kitchen)

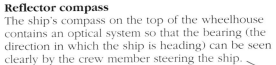

Skipper's accommodation

Mate's accommodation

Crew accommodation

Anchor windlass
A power windlass (winch) hauls in the anchor when the ship moves from the fishing grounds.

Anchor
The ship has two anchors — one each side of the hull.

Anchor windlass machinery

Anchor chain locker
The long anchor chain is stored in here when it is hauled in by the windlass.

Water ballast tank
When the ship is not fully loaded, water in the ballast tank keeps it on an even keel (level in the sea). As the crew catch and load fish, water is pumped out of the ballast to compensate for the extra weight on board.

Rib construction
The ship must be strong to withstand the ice and high seas of the Arctic fishing grounds. So the steel plates of the hull are welded to a structure of ribs.

Fresh water tanks

Chart room
Ocean maps are called charts. They show the coastline, depth of the water, and features such as lighthouses.

Oil tanks

Engine control room
Sound insulation absorbs the noise from the engines so the control room is fairly quiet.

Recreation room

Messroom
The crew snatch meals in the messroom during breaks in the fishing.

Electronics room
Fishing vessels have many navigational aids. Electronic instruments monitor signals from land beacons or orbiting satellites to give the ship's position to within about 100 m. Sonar and echo sounding equipment help the crew locate schools of fish.

Boiler

Fuel oil tanks

Engine room
The 2,500-horsepower main engine can power the ship forward at up to 14 knots (14 nautical mph).

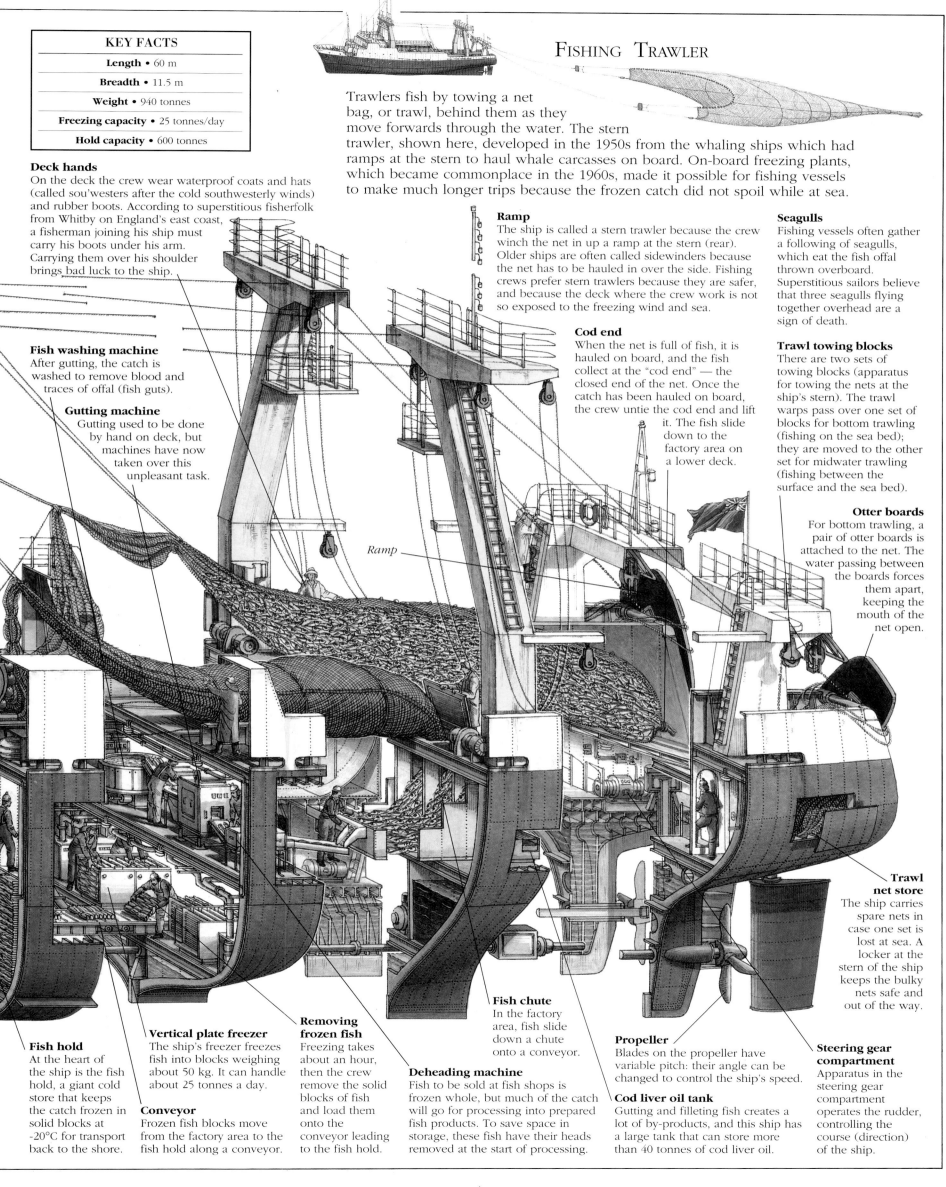

KEY FACTS	
Length • 60 m	
Breadth • 11.5 m	
Weight • 940 tonnes	
Freezing capacity • 25 tonnes/day	
Hold capacity • 600 tonnes	

FISHING TRAWLER

Trawlers fish by towing a net bag, or trawl, behind them as they move forwards through the water. The stern trawler, shown here, developed in the 1950s from the whaling ships which had ramps at the stern to haul whale carcasses on board. On-board freezing plants, which became commonplace in the 1960s, made it possible for fishing vessels to make much longer trips because the frozen catch did not spoil while at sea.

Deck hands
On the deck the crew wear waterproof coats and hats (called sou'westers after the cold southwesterly winds) and rubber boots. According to superstitious fisherfolk from Whitby on England's east coast, a fisherman joining his ship must carry his boots under his arm. Carrying them over his shoulder brings bad luck to the ship.

Fish washing machine
After gutting, the catch is washed to remove blood and traces of offal (fish guts).

Gutting machine
Gutting used to be done by hand on deck, but machines have now taken over this unpleasant task.

Ramp
The ship is called a stern trawler because the crew winch the net in up a ramp at the stern (rear). Older ships are often called sidewinders because the net has to be hauled in over the side. Fishing crews prefer stern trawlers because they are safer, and because the deck where the crew work is not so exposed to the freezing wind and sea.

Cod end
When the net is full of fish, it is hauled on board, and the fish collect at the "cod end" — the closed end of the net. Once the catch has been hauled on board, the crew untie the cod end and lift it. The fish slide down to the factory area on a lower deck.

Ramp

Seagulls
Fishing vessels often gather a following of seagulls, which eat the fish offal thrown overboard. Superstitious sailors believe that three seagulls flying together overhead are a sign of death.

Trawl towing blocks
There are two sets of towing blocks (apparatus for towing the nets at the ship's stern). The trawl warps pass over one set of blocks for bottom trawling (fishing on the sea bed); they are moved to the other set for midwater trawling (fishing between the surface and the sea bed).

Otter boards
For bottom trawling, a pair of otter boards is attached to the net. The water passing between the boards forces them apart, keeping the mouth of the net open.

Trawl net store
The ship carries spare nets in case one set is lost at sea. A locker at the stern of the ship keeps the bulky nets safe and out of the way.

Fish hold
At the heart of the ship is the fish hold, a giant cold store that keeps the catch frozen in solid blocks at -20°C for transport back to the shore.

Vertical plate freezer
The ship's freezer freezes fish into blocks weighing about 50 kg. It can handle about 25 tonnes a day.

Conveyor
Frozen fish blocks move from the factory area to the fish hold along a conveyor.

Removing frozen fish
Freezing takes about an hour, then the crew remove the solid blocks of fish and load them onto the conveyor leading to the fish hold.

Fish chute
In the factory area, fish slide down a chute onto a conveyor.

Deheading machine
Fish to be sold at fish shops is frozen whole, but much of the catch will go for processing into prepared fish products. To save space in storage, these fish have their heads removed at the start of processing.

Propeller
Blades on the propeller have variable pitch: their angle can be changed to control the ship's speed.

Cod liver oil tank
Gutting and filleting fish creates a lot of by-products, and this ship has a large tank that can store more than 40 tonnes of cod liver oil.

Steering gear compartment
Apparatus in the steering gear compartment operates the rudder, controlling the course (direction) of the ship.

EMPIRE STATE BUILDING

Not long ago, cities looked very different, because until about 1880 few buildings rose higher than about five floors. One reason for this was the stairs: nobody wanted to walk any higher. Another obstacle was the thickness of the walls, which had to support the great weight of the building. In addition, businesses were generally small, and there was no real demand for tall buildings to house them. The invention of the safety elevator (lift) by Elisha Otis (1811-1861) in 1852 solved the first problem. The second was solved when stronger steel replaced weaker cast iron starting in the 1870s. It then became possible to give buildings a strong frame to carry the weight of every floor. The walls no longer took the weight, so they could be thin and light, or even made of glass. The skyscraper was born!

Office space
To ensure that natural daylight reaches everywhere, no office space is further than 8.5 m from a window. This was a rule laid down when the building was commissioned (ordered) and the architect took great care to follow it. The appearance of the Empire State Building might have been very different if bigger rooms had been allowed.

Central service core
Much of the ingenuity that went into the design of the building was spent planning the central core that rises from the ground to the top floor. The core carries the lifts and all the services, such as electricity, telephones, air conditioning, and plumbing.

Postal room
The building is so vast that it needs its own post office. Here in the postal room, workers sort post that is delivered by chutes from every floor.

Piles
More than 200 piles (columns driven into the ground) support the weight of the Empire State Building. The piles, made of steel and concrete, rest directly on the bedrock 10 m below street level.

Bedrock
New York was the original skyscraper city. Manhattan Island at its centre is made of granite, which provides a solid foundation for the many massively heavy buildings.

Stairs
There are 1,860 steps from street level to the 102nd floor.

Inter-floor structure
Floors are constructed like sandwiches, with space in between for cables, telephone lines, and pipes.

Foundation level
To dig the foundations, workers removed rock and soil amounting to three quarters of the weight of the Empire State Building itself.

Observatory
From the viewing platform on the 102nd floor, visitors can see more than 125 km on a clear day. Two million people a year come to see the view, but many are disappointed, because mist often shrouds the building.

Observation windows
Because high winds sweep upwards around the building, visitors sometimes see rain and snow falling upwards.

Airship mooring mast
The original owners of the Empire State Building planned an airship mooring mast for the top. In the days before passenger aircraft, everyone thought that airships (huge passenger balloons) would soon be flying regularly from Europe to the United States. However, landing airships on the mast proved to be highly dangerous, and the idea was abandoned.

Express lifts
The fastest lifts whisk sight-seers to the observation galleries at speeds of more than 350 m a minute.

Cleaners
The window cleaners work from cradles that hang from winches running around the roof of the 80th floor. Each of the building's 6,500 windows are cleaned every month. The job is made more difficult by high winds which make the water trickle up the window instead of down.

TV mast
The tip of the 67-m TV mast that tops off the Empire State Building is 449 m above the ground.

lift motors

Water
To raise water to the top of the building requires pumps with tremendous power. 100 km of pipe channel the water from the pumps to every floor.

Electrical switchgear
Tenants of the building consume enough power every year to supply a city of 11,000 inhabitants. There are transformers in the basement and on the 84th floor.

Storage areas

Lift motors
The positioning of the lifts was vital to the building's success. Too few lifts, and tenants could not get to their offices quickly enough. But each new lift reduces the amount of office space to let. In the end, 73 lifts were built.

Steel floor frame
A network of horizontal steel girders built first provided a firm support for the concrete floors that were poured on top, and left to harden. Even at the time the frame was unnecessarily heavy — today only half the weight of steel would be used.

Curtain wall
The Empire State Building was designed as a framework, with an outside shell called a curtain wall to keep the weather out and the people in. Most of the wall panels were prefabricated — cut to size or assembled elsewhere — so that they could be installed rapidly.

Concrete floor

Beacons
The Empire State Building has beacons to warn aircraft of its height, but on 28 July 1945 a fog-bound plane crashed into the building between the 78th and 79th floors. A typewriter mechanic, Alf Spalthoff, saw the crash as he ate a tuna sandwich in a café not far away. He said: "When it hit there was a big explosion that seemed to come from four or five of the floors at once."

Wall panels
The shimmering vertical lines of the building's exterior are created by stainless-steel panels. The lines draw the eye upwards, making the building look taller.

Brick lining
When the curtain wall was fixed in place, workers lined the inside of each floor with bricks — ten million of them for the whole building.

Lobby
Inside the main door, a magnificent lobby rises three storeys high. On the walls are paintings of the seven great wonders of the world — and one of the Empire State Building, which the owners modestly claimed was the eighth wonder, and the only one built in the 20th century.

Office workers
15,000 people work in the Empire State Building.

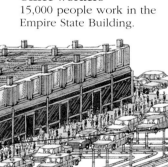

TALL TALE
The Empire State Building in New York City, United States, is the world's best-known skyscraper. Opened on 1 May 1931, it was for many years the world's tallest building. It was the creation of a group of business tycoons led by John Jacob Raskob. His aim was to commission the most beautiful skyscraper ever built — but also to make a lot of money by renting out the office space in the building, which stands on one of the city's most desirable sites.

Get it up quick
The Empire State Building was completed in record time: 3,000 workers laboured daily for less than 15 months to finish it. But in the rush to construct the building, 14 workers died in accidents.

Tenants' offices
The Empire State Building is an office block, with office space rented out to tenants. When the building opened during the Great Depression, business in the United States was very bad, and the owners were at first able to rent only a quarter of the offices. New Yorkers dubbed it "The Empty State Building".

Power cables
More than 600 km of cable supply power and light to office tenants.

Main entrance
The Empire State Building is constructed so that the main door opens onto Fifth Avenue, New York's most fashionable street.

Utilities
Conduits, pipes, and cables under the street supply the building with gas, phone lines, water, steam, and electricity.

Car parking

Electrical gear

Steel skeleton
Building the Empire State Building's supporting framework required 58,000 tonnes of steel. 300 steelworkers completed the frame in 23 weeks.

Building materials
If a single train had brought all the building materials to the site, the guard's van would have been more than 90 km away when the engine arrived.

Cleaners
When the office workers have gone home, 150 cleaners vacuum and dust.

Air conditioning
Large buildings would be uncomfortable to work in without special heating and ventilation systems. The Empire State Building is air conditioned by more than 5,000 tonnes of equipment in the basement, which pumps chilled water to air conditioning units in every office. The air inside the building changes six times an hour.

Waste disposal plant
Cleaners empty waste paper into sacks, and carry it to the basement in the service elevators. The waste is stored for a day in case someone throws valuable papers away, and needs to sort through the rubbish. After 24 hours, the waste is compacted into bales weighing nearly half a tonne, and removed.

KEY FACTS

Height • 449 m (including TV mast)
Weight • 308,000 tonnes
Ground area • 7,780 square m
Volume • 1.05 million cubic m
Floors • 102
Stairs to top • 1,860

SPACE SHUTTLE

For centuries, people have dreamed of space travel. The dream came true in 1961 when space flights with human crews began. But soon the dream became a nightmare. Space vehicles are very expensive. And only a tiny part of each returned to Earth. The rest remained in orbit (floating weightless in space) as hazardous "space junk".

The space shuttle solves these problems because it is the first re-useable space vehicle. Like other spacecraft, the shuttle escapes Earth's gravity (the pulling force that gives everything its weight) on the back of a rocket. But the shuttle soars back to Earth like a glider, to be used again.

Where's the bath?
Washing is not easy on the orbiter because without gravity water can't flow down; instead it goes everywhere, and can damage delicate equipment. To wash hands, there's a device like a goldfish bowl. A constant flow of air through the hand-holes controls the water inside.

To wash faces and bodies the crew use flannels.

Heatproof tiles
When the orbiter re-enters the Earth's atmosphere, the friction (rubbing) of the air rushing past slows it down. However, the friction heats the orbiter to a very high temperature. To protect the craft, it is covered in 24,192 ceramic heatproof tiles. Each is individually made, and no two tiles are the same.

Taking up arms
Because there is no gravity in space, a delicately jointed arm can do jobs that would require a huge crane on Earth. The remote manipulator arm moves in many directions, so that it can lift satellites and other payloads (cargoes) in the cargo bay.

Payload assist module
A small rocket engine, called the payload assist module, powers the satellite into a higher orbit as soon as it is a safe distance from the orbiter.

Radiator
The apparatus on board the orbiter generates a large amount of heat. A cooling system similar to that in a refrigerator takes the heat to radiators fixed to the cargo bay doors. From there, the heat disperses into space.

THE SHUTTLE ORBITER

The section of the space shuttle housing the crew and cargo compartments is called the orbiter. At launch the orbiter is dwarfed by a huge external fuel tank, and two solid-fuel rocket boosters. The orbiter discards these parts less than 10 minutes after leaving the ground.

Vertical stabilizer
Like the fin of an aircraft, the vertical stabilizer keeps the shuttle on course in the Earth's atmosphere, and helps it steer.

Main engine nozzle
Burning liquid hydrogen and oxygen in these nozzles gives the orbiter the power it needs to lift off into space. After lift off these engines are not used again on the mission.

Rear rockets
External pods on either side of the orbiter fuselage contain the rocket engines and fuel supply that the craft uses to manoeuvre (change speed and position) in space.

Orbital manoeuvring system (OMS) engines
The crew fire the OMS engines to make major changes to the orbiter's speed and direction in space.

Smart system
The reaction control system (RCS) makes small changes in the position of the orbiter. There are 44 small rocket engines fired by the autopilot. Tiny engines called vernier thrusters fine tune space manoeuvres.

Fuel and oxidizer supplies
Ball-shaped tanks hold the fuel for the OMS and RCS engines. In addition to the fuel tank there is a separate supply of oxidizer — without this, the fuel would not burn.

Wing sections
The orbiter's wings are constructed in a similar way to those of an aircraft, with a framework of aluminium spars and ribs.

Auxiliary power unit fuel

Cargo bay door

Going down?
When the orbiter is landing, the crew use movable sections of the wing, called elevons, to control the craft's glide back to the ground.

Wonderful wheels
As the orbiter approaches the landing site, the pilot presses a button on the flightdeck to extend the landing gear (landing wheels).

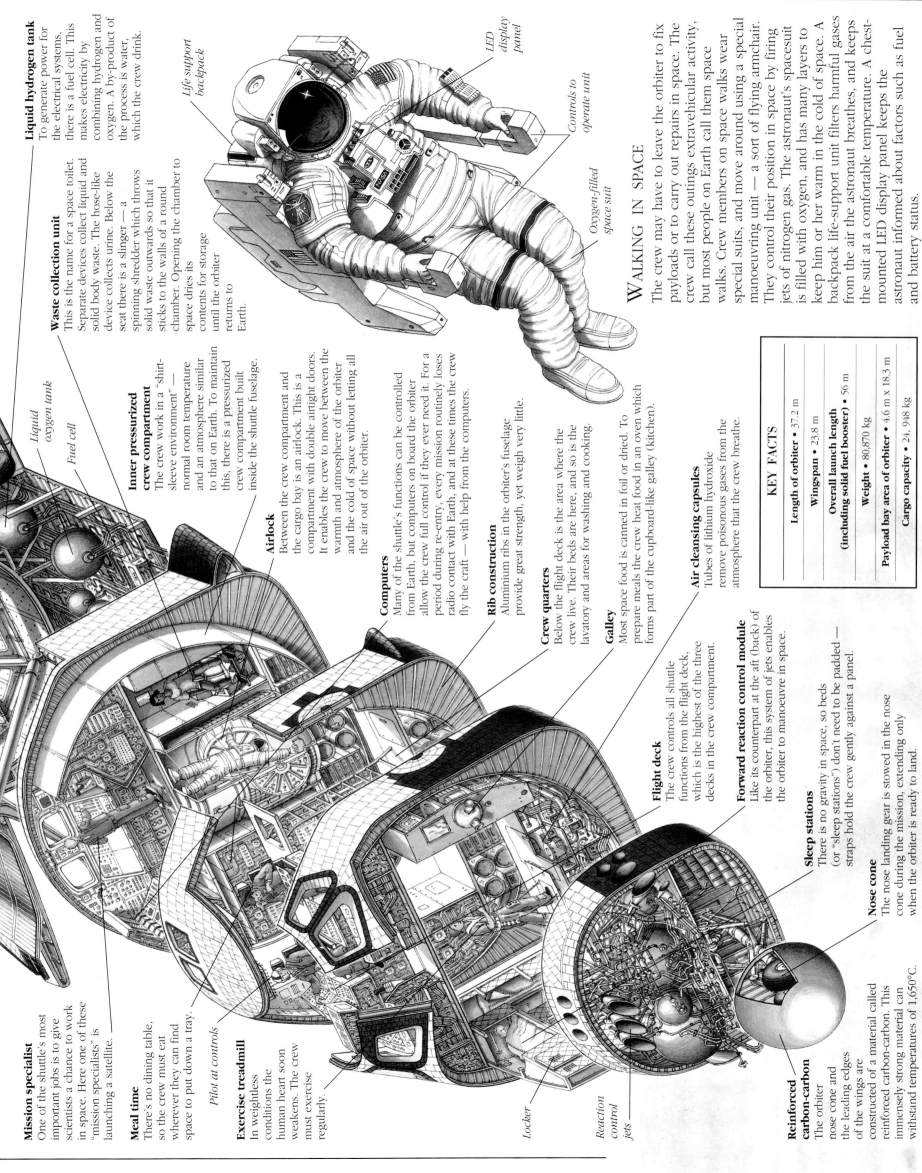

Liquid hydrogen tank
To generate power for the electrical systems, there is a fuel cell. This makes electricity by combining hydrogen and oxygen. A by-product of the process is water, which the crew drink.

Liquid oxygen tank

Fuel cell

Life support backpack

LED display panel

Controls to operate unit

Oxygen-filled space suit

Waste collection unit
This is the name for a space toilet. Separate devices collect liquid and solid body waste. The hose-like device collects urine. Below the seat there is a slinger — a spinning shredder which throws solid waste outwards so that it sticks to the walls of a round chamber. Opening the chamber to space dries its contents for storage until the orbiter returns to Earth.

Inner pressurized crew compartment
The crew work in a "shirt-sleeve environment" — normal room temperature and an atmosphere similar to that on Earth. To maintain this, there is a pressurized crew compartment built inside the shuttle fuselage.

Airlock
Between the crew compartment and the cargo bay is an airlock. This is a compartment with double airtight doors. It enables the crew to move between the warmth and atmosphere of the orbiter and the cold of space without letting all the air out of the orbiter.

Computers
Many of the shuttle's functions can be controlled from Earth, but computers on board the orbiter allow the crew full control if they ever need it. For a period during re-entry, every mission routinely loses radio contact with Earth, and at these times the crew fly the craft — with help from the computers.

Rib construction
Aluminium ribs in the orbiter's fuselage provide great strength, yet weigh very little.

Crew quarters
Below the flight deck is the area where the crew live. Their beds are here, and so is the lavatory and areas for washing and cooking.

Galley
Most space food is canned in foil or dried. To prepare meals the crew heat food in an oven which forms part of the cupboard-like galley (kitchen).

Air cleansing capsules
Tubes of lithium hydroxide remove poisonous gases from the atmosphere that the crew breathe.

Walking in space

The crew may have to leave the orbiter to fix payloads or to carry out repairs in space. The crew call these outings extravehicular activity, but most people on Earth call them space walks. Crew members on space walks wear special suits, and move around using a special manoeuvring unit — a sort of flying armchair. They control their position in space by firing jets of nitrogen gas. The astronaut's spacesuit is filled with oxygen, and has many layers to keep him or her warm in the cold of space. A backpack life-support unit filters harmful gases from the air the astronaut breathes, and keeps the suit at a comfortable temperature. A chest-mounted LED display panel keeps the astronaut informed about factors such as fuel and battery status.

KEY FACTS	
Length of orbiter • 37.2 m	
Wingspan • 23.8 m	
Overall launch length (including solid fuel booster) • 56 m	
Weight • 80,870 kg	
Payload bay area of orbiter • 4.6 m x 18.3 m	
Cargo capacity • 24,948 kg	

Mission specialist
One of the shuttle's most important jobs is to give scientists a chance to work in space. Here one of these "mission specialists" is launching a satellite.

Meal time
There's no dining table, so the crew must eat wherever they can find space to put down a tray.

Pilot at controls

Exercise treadmill
In weightless conditions the human heart soon weakens. The crew must exercise regularly.

Locker

Reaction control jets

Reinforced carbon-carbon
The orbiter nose cone and the leading edges of the wings are constructed of a material called reinforced carbon-carbon. This immensely strong material can withstand temperatures of 1,650°C.

Flight deck
The crew controls all shuttle functions from the flight deck, which is the highest of the three decks in the crew compartment.

Forward reaction control module
Like its counterpart at the aft (back) of the orbiter, this system of jets enables the orbiter to manoeuvre in space.

Sleep stations
There is no gravity in space, so beds (or 'sleep stations') don't need to be padded — straps hold the crew gently against a panel.

Nose cone
The nose landing gear is stowed in the nose cone during the mission, extending only when the orbiter is ready to land.

INDEX

Acknowledgments

Dorling Kindersley would like to thank the following individuals and organizations for their help in the preparation of this book:

Janet Abbott
Boeing International Corporation
BP Exploration UK Limited
Lynn Bresler
British Coal Corporation
British Interplanetary Society
Cunard Line Limited
Robin Kerrod
London Underground Limited
Dr. Anne Millard
The Science Museum
Andrew Smith
Martin Taylor
Westland Group plc